Contents

KV-236-583

Introduction   *4*

Test 1   Reading and Use of English   *8*
             Writing   *20*
             Listening   *22*
             Speaking   *28*

Test 2   Reading and Use of English   *30*
             Writing   *42*
             Listening   *44*
             Speaking   *50*

Test 3   Reading and Use of English   *52*
             Writing   *64*
             Listening   *66*
             Speaking   *72*

Test 4   Reading and Use of English   *74*
             Writing   *86*
             Listening   *88*
             Speaking   *94*

Sample answer sheets   *95*

Thanks and acknowledgements   *103*

Visual materials for the Speaking test   *colour section*

ESOL, Access & Progression

Introduction

This collection of four complete practice tests comprises papers from the *Cambridge English: First (FCE)* examination; students can practise these tests on their own or with the help of a teacher.

   The *Cambridge English: First* examination is part of a suite of general English examinations produced by Cambridge English Language Assessment. This suite consists of five examinations that have similar characteristics but are designed for different levels of English language ability. Within the five levels, *Cambridge English: First* is at Level B2 in the Council of Europe's *Common European Framework of Reference for Languages: Learning, teaching, assessment*. It has also been accredited by Ofqual, the statutory regulatory authority in England, at Level 1 in the National Qualifications Framework. The *Cambridge English: First* examination is widely recognised in commerce and industry, and in individual university faculties and other educational institutions.

Examination	Council of Europe Framework Level	UK National Qualifications Framework Level
Cambridge English: Proficiency *Certificate of Proficiency in English (CPE)*	C2	3
Cambridge English: Advanced *Certificate in Advanced English (CAE)*	C1	2
Cambridge English: First *First Certificate in English (FCE)*	B2	1
Cambridge English: Preliminary *Preliminary English Test (PET)*	B1	Entry 3
Cambridge English: Key *Key English Test (KET)*	A2	Entry 2

Further information

The information contained in this practice book is designed to be an overview of the exam. For a full description of all of the above exams, including information about task types, testing focus and preparation, please see the relevant handbooks which can be obtained from Cambridge English Language Assessment at the address below or from the website at:
www.CambridgeEnglish.org

Cambridge English Language Assessment
1 Hills Road
Cambridge CB1 2EU
United Kingdom

Telephone: +44 1223 553997
Fax: +44 1223 553621
email: helpdesk@cambridgeenglish.org

Cambridge English

OFFICIAL

Esol Access & Progression

FIRST 1

FIRST CERTIFICATE IN ENGLISH

WITHOUT ANSWERS

AUTHENTIC EXAMINATION PAPERS
FROM CAMBRIDGE ENGLISH
LANGUAGE ASSESSMENT

For revised exam from 2015

Cambridge University Press
www.cambridge.org/elt

Cambridge English Language Assessment
www.cambridgeenglish.org

Information on this title: www.cambridge.org/9781107668577

© Cambridge University Press and UCLES 2014

First published 2014
4th printing 2015

Printed in Italy by Rotolito Lombarda S.p.A.

A catalogue record for this publication is available from the British Library

ISBN 978-1-107-69591-7 Student's Book with answers
ISBN 978-1-107-66857-7 Student's Book without answers
ISBN 978-1-107-69448-4 Audio CDs (2)
ISBN 978-1-107-66331-2 Student's Book Pack (Student's Book with answers and Audio CDs (2))

The structure of *Cambridge English: First* – an overview

The *Cambridge English: First* examination consists of four papers.

Reading and Use of English   1 hour 15 minutes
This paper consists of **seven parts**, with 52 questions. For Parts 1 to 4, the test contains texts with accompanying grammar and vocabulary tasks, and separate items with a grammar and vocabulary focus. For Parts 5 to 7, the test contains a range of texts and accompanying reading comprehension tasks.

Writing   1 hour 20 minutes
This paper consists of **two parts** which carry equal marks. In Part 1, which is **compulsory**, candidates have to write an essay of between 140 and 190 words, giving their opinion in response to a task. In Part 2, there are three tasks from which candidates choose **one** to write about. The range of tasks from which questions may be drawn includes an article, an email/letter, a report and a review. In this part, candidates have to write between 140 and 190 words.

Listening   40 minutes (approximately)
This paper consists of **four parts**. Each part contains a recorded text or texts and some questions, including multiple-choice, sentence completion and multiple-matching questions.
Each text is heard twice. There is a total of **30 questions**.

Speaking   14 minutes
This paper consists of **four parts**. The standard test format is two candidates and two examiners. One examiner takes part in the conversation while the other examiner listens. Both examiners give marks. Candidates will be given photographs and other visual and written material to look at and talk about. Sometimes candidates will talk with the other candidate, sometimes with the examiner, and sometimes with both.

Grading

The overall Cambridge English: First grade is based on the total score gained in all four papers. All candidates receive a Statement of Results which includes a profile of their performance in each of the four skills and Use of English. Certificates are given to candidates who pass the examination with grade A, B or C. Candidates who achieve grade A receive the Cambridge English: First certificate stating that they demonstrated ability at Level C1. Candidates whose performance is below level B2, but falls within Level B1, receive a Cambridge English certificate stating that they have demonstrated ability a Level B1. Candidates whose performance falls below Level Bl do not receive a certificate.

   For further information on grading and results, go to the website (see page 4).

Test 1

READING AND USE OF ENGLISH (1 hour 15 minutes)

Part 1

For questions **1–8**, read the text below and decide which answer (**A, B, C** or **D**) best fits each gap. There is an example at the beginning (**0**).

Mark your answers **on the separate answer sheet**.

Example:

0   A have   **B** do   **C** get   **D** take

0	A	B	C	D
	▄	▭	▭	▭

Why we need to play

Human beings are not the only creatures that like to **(0)** .... fun. Many animals play, as do some birds. However, no other creatures spend so much time enjoying themselves as human beings do. Indeed, we **(1)** .... onto our sense of fun right into adulthood.

So why do human beings spend so much time playing? One reason is that we have time for leisure; animals have very little time to play as most of their life is spent sleeping and **(2)** .... food.

So, is play just an opportunity for us to **(3)** .... in enjoyable activities or does it have a more important **(4)** .... ? According to scientists, **(5)** .... from being fun, play has several very real **(6)** .... for us – it helps our physical, intellectual and social development. It also helps to **(7)** .... us for what we have not yet experienced. With very **(8)** .... risk, we can act out what we would do in unexpected, or even dangerous, situations.

1	**A** hold	**B** keep	**C** save	**D** stay
2	**A** searching	**B** looking	**C** seeking	**D** gaining
3	**A** engage	**B** combine	**C** contribute	**D** involve
4	**A** motive	**B** purpose	**C** intention	**D** cause
5	**A** excluding	**B** except	**C** apart	**D** away
6	**A** assets	**B** profits	**C** services	**D** benefits
7	**A** plan	**B** prepare	**C** practise	**D** provide
8	**A** brief	**B** short	**C** narrow	**D** little

Part 2

For questions **9–16**, read the text below and think of the word which best fits each gap. Use only **one** word in each gap. There is an example at the beginning (**0**).

Write your answers **IN CAPITAL LETTERS on the separate answer sheet.**

Example: | **0** | *B* | *E* | *E* | *N* | | | | | | | | | | | | | |

A bicycle you can fold up

Folding bicycles have **(0)** ……... around for quite some time now. However, an amazing new Japanese version **(9)** ……... be folded with a swiftness and efficiency never seen before. This bike is designed **(10)** ……... that it is possible to fold it up quickly. Once folded, you pull the bike along **(11)** ……... ease.

This remarkable bike has a half-folding frame with a hinge in the middle. And, although the basic idea is **(12)** ……... original, its inventor has created an especially clever variation, combining compactness **(13)** ……... convenience with smart design.

Recently, folding bicycles **(14)** ……... become very popular in Japan, particularly in congested urban areas like Tokyo, a city **(15)** ……... every square centimetre of space is in great demand. Japanese cyclists need to be able to store their bikes in tiny areas at home or the office. And **(16)** ……... they should want to take their bicycle on the underground, a folding model is a big advantage.

Part 3

For questions **17–24**, read the text below. Use the word given in capitals at the end of some of the lines to form a word that fits in the gap **in the same line**. There is an example at the beginning (**0**).

Write your answers **IN CAPITAL LETTERS on the separate answer sheet**.

Example: | 0 | E | X | T | R | E | M | E | L | Y | | | | | | | | |

Tea

Tea is an (**0**) .... popular drink with many people. It is estimated that **EXTREME**

the consumption of tea in England alone exceeds 165 million cups daily.

Despite this, the drink was virtually (**17**) .... in England until about **KNOW**

400 years ago. The first (**18**) .... to tea in England comes in a **REFER**

diary written in 1660. However, its (**19**) .... really took off after the **POPULAR**

(**20**) .... of King Charles II to Catherine of Braganza. It was her great **MARRY**

love of tea that made it (**21**) .... **FASHION**

It was believed that tea was good for people as it seemed to be capable

of reviving the spirits and curing certain minor (**22**) .... It has even **ILL**

been suggested by some historians that it played a significant part in the

Industrial Revolution. Tea, they say, increased the number of hours that

(**23**) .... could work in factories as the caffeine in tea made them more **LABOUR**

(**24**) .... and consequently able to work longer hours. **ENERGY**

Part 4

For questions **25–30**, complete the second sentence so that it has a similar meaning to the first sentence, using the word given. **Do not change the word given.** You must use between **two** and **five** words, including the word given. Here is an example (**0**).

Example:

0   A very friendly taxi driver drove us into town.

DRIVEN

We .... a very friendly taxi driver.

The gap can be filled by the words 'were driven into town by', so you write:

Example:	0	*WERE DRIVEN INTO TOWN BY*

Write **only** the missing words **IN CAPITAL LETTERS on the separate answer sheet**.

---

25   They didn't sell many programmes at the match.

FEW

Very .... at the match last Saturday.

26   We got to work late because we decided to drive rather than take the train.

INSTEAD

We got to work late because we decided to drive .... the train.

27   Last Friday was the first time my car ever broke down, even though it is very old.

NEVER

Until last Friday, my car .... down, even though it is very old.

28   'All your complaints will be investigated by my staff tomorrow,' said the bank manager.

   LOOK

   The bank manager promised that his staff .... all our complaints the next day.

29   Last year the heavy rain caused the postponement of the tennis tournament.

   BECAUSE

   Last year the tennis tournament .... so heavily.

30   Jack does not want to work for his uncle any longer.

   CARRY

   John does not want .... for his uncle.

Part 5

You are going to read a magazine article about a famous pianist and the young student who became his pupil. For questions **31–36**, choose the answer (**A, B, C** or **D**) which you think fits best according to the text.

Mark your answers **on the separate answer sheet**.

A musician and his pupil

Paul Williams interviews the famous pianist Alfred Brendel.

Over six decades the pianist Alfred Brendel gradually built up and maintained a dominant position in the world of classical music. He was an intellectual, sometimes austere, figure who explored and recorded the mainstream European works for the piano. He wrote and played a great deal, but taught very little. Those who knew him best glimpsed a playful side to his character, but that was seldom on display in his concerts. It was a disciplined, never-ending cycle of study, travel and performance.

And then, four or five years ago, a young boy, Kit Armstrong, appeared backstage at one of Brendel's concerts and asked for lessons. Initially, Brendel didn't take the suggestion very seriously. He had had very few pupils and he saw no reason to start now. He quotes from another famous pianist: 'You don't employ a mountain guide to teach a child how to walk.' But there was something that struck him about the young boy – then about 14. He listened to him play. Brendel explained, 'He played remarkably well and by heart. Then he brought me a CD of a little recital he had given where he played so beautifully that I thought to myself, "I have to make time for him." It was a performance that really led you from the first to the last note. It's very rare to find any musician with this kind of overview and the necessary subtlety.'

As Brendel is bowing out of the public eye, so Kit is nudging his way into it – restrained by Brendel, ever nervous about the young man burning out early. Kit, now 19, is a restless, impatient presence away from the lessons – always learning new languages; taking himself off to study maths, writing computer code or playing tennis. All under the watchful eye of his ever-present mother. On top of all this he composes. 'This was very important,' Brendel says. 'If you want to learn to read music properly it is helped by the fact that you try to write something yourself. Then I noticed that Kit had a phenomenal memory and that he was a phenomenal sight reader. But more than this is his ability to listen to his own playing, his sensitivity to sound and his ability to listen to me when I try to explain something. He not only usually understands what I mean, but he can do it. And when I tell him one thing in a piece, he will do it everywhere in the piece where it comes in later.'

Brendel catches himself and looks at me severely. *line 50* 'Now I don't want to raise any expectations. I'm very cross if some newspapers try to do this. There was one article which named him as the future great pianist of the 21st century, I mean, really, it's the worst thing. One doesn't say that in a newspaper. And it has done a great deal of harm. As usual, with gifted young players, he can play certain things amazingly well, while others need more time and experience. It would be harmful if a critic was there expecting the greatest perfection.'

It is touching to see the mellowness of Brendel in his post-performing years. He explains 'When I was very young, I didn't have the urge to be famous in five years' time, but I had the idea I would like to have done certain things by the age of 50. And when I was 50, I thought that I had done most of those things, but there was still some leeway for more, so I went on. Although I do not have the physical power to play now, in my head, there are always things going on, all sorts of pieces that I've never played. I don't play now but it's a very nice new career.'

31 What is the writer emphasising in the first paragraph?

    A the wide range of music that Brendel has played
    B the total dedication of Brendel to his art
    C the reluctance of Brendel to take on pupils
    D the light-hearted nature of Brendel's character

32 Brendel uses the quotation about the mountain guide to illustrate that

    A it is not always easy to teach people the basics.
    B it is unwise to try to teach new skills before people are ready.
    C people can learn new skills without help from others.
    D it is unnecessary for an expert to teach people the basics.

33 What made Brendel first decide to accept Kit as a pupil?

    A He seemed so young and serious.
    B He was so determined and persistent.
    C He could play without the music.
    D He had an extraordinary talent.

34 Which of Kit's musical abilities does Brendel admire the most?

    A He is able to write music himself.
    B He is able to understand and respond to advice.
    C He can play a piece of music the first time he sees it.
    D He is able to remember all the music he has ever played.

35 Why does the writer use the phrase 'catches himself' in line 50?

    A He realises he has said too much to a journalist.
    B He doesn't enjoy giving interviews to journalists.
    C He wants to be careful he doesn't upset any music critics.
    D He resents the way that he has often been misquoted.

36 What is Brendel doing in the final paragraph?

    A justifying his lack of ambition when he was young
    B expressing regret at the loss of his physical strength
    C describing his present state of mind
    D explaining which pieces he prefers to play now

Part 6

You are going to read a newspaper article about a blind runner. Six sentences have been removed from the article. Choose from the sentences **A–G** the one which fits each gap (**37–42**). There is one extra sentence which you do not need to use.

Mark your answers **on the separate answer sheet**.

Blind Runner

Paul Hardy reports on a blind runner called Simon Wheatcroft who enjoys taking part in marathon and ultra-marathon races, running distances between 42 km and 160 km.

Running marathons, a race of 42 km, has become increasingly popular. This distance poses extreme physical and mental challenges for anyone, but for Simon Wheatcroft there is another hurdle; he has been blind since he was 18 years old.

For the past two years Simon, now 29, has been overcoming his disability to compete in marathons and ultra-marathons by training with runners who act as his guides, and also, rather uniquely, by teaching himself to run solo, out on the streets. 'I got bored exercising indoors, so thought, "I'll have a go at running outside",' he explains. **37** Then he got bored again and wanted to try running on the roads.

Weeks of gradual exploration followed, walking a route alone. **38** It took him along little-used pavements alongside a busy main road. He also recruited technology to help him form his mental map of the area using a smartphone app, to provide feedback through headphones about his pace and distance. This information could then be cross-referenced with his knowledge of the route and any obstacles.

Now, having covered hundreds of km alone on the route, Simon has been able, gradually, to phase out the app. 'When I first started I had to really concentrate to an unbelievable level to know where my feet were falling. Now it has become quite automated.' **39** 'I did make a few mistakes early on – like running into

posts. But you only run into a post once before you think "Right. I'm going to remember where that is next time",' he laughs.

Joining Simon for a training session, it's striking how natural and fluid his movement is; he takes shorter, shallower, more gentle steps than most runners, using his feet to feel his way. His landmarks are minute changes in gradient and slight variations in the running surface. **40** 'I have to believe this route is going to stay consistent, and there won't be things like roadwork signs or big rocks,' he says.

41 'I try to concentrate on the millions of footsteps that go right and think positively,' he explains. When it comes to racing in ultra-distance events, Simon has to use guides to run sections of the course with him; after all, it would be almost impossible to memorise a 150 km stretch of countryside by heart. However, the physical and practical advantages of training in the fresh air, on his own terms, are vast and have boosted his confidence in his running ability as well as providing inspiration to others.

But for Simon the real thrill and motivation for training come from simply being able to compete on equal terms. **42** 'I can't hide the fact I'm blind,' he says, 'but at the same time I would rather compete with everybody else and not be put into a special group. Being visually impaired doesn't mean you can't run.'

16

A These provide the familiarity and consistency essential for the blind runner.

B Their support gave him extra confidence regarding his changing surroundings.

C Simon believes the feelings of liberation and independence he gets from running solo far outweigh any anxiety over such dangers.

D He began by training on football pitches behind his house, running between the goalposts.

E It gives him a great opportunity to run with everyone.

F That's not to say the learning curve has been without incident.

G As a result of this slow experimentation, he was able to memorise a set five-kilometre course.

Part 7

You are going to read an article in which four graduates discuss going to university. For questions **43–52**, choose from the graduates (**A–D**). The graduates may be chosen more than once.

Mark your answers **on the separate answer sheet**.

Which graduate

says people should be allowed to consider a range of options apart from university?	**43**
says that some people are expected to make important decisions before they are ready?	**44**
initially rejected something she was told?	**45**
was unaware of the alternatives to university?	**46**
says that the type of learning at university is different from that at other institutions?	**47**
felt when she was a student that she might not be doing the right course?	**48**
says that some people discover that what is studied at university is not useful in the workplace?	**49**
was uncertain about her reasons for going to university?	**50**
says graduates have an advantage when applying for jobs?	**51**
was expected to go to university despite being a fairly average student at school?	**52**

Why go to university?

Four graduates talk about their experiences.

A   Sonia

While I was doing my physics degree people would often say I was acquiring skills I'd be able to use in my future career, even if I didn't become a physicist. It sounded like nonsense to me: if I did another job in the end, what could be relevant about knowing what's inside an atom or how to operate a laser? It turns out they were referring to the wealth of other skills you pick up along the way. Communication and problem-solving are just two of these. In contrast to the way you may have been taught before, university teaches you to be innovative and to think for yourself. Going to university is about more than just studying though! I got to make friends from all over the world and they have proved to be useful work contacts.

B   Jane

I went to university because it was the career path expected by school, parents and classmates (to an extent) and also because I didn't really have a clue about what other options were open to me. It's difficult to know how things would have turned out if I hadn't gone. I do know that the job I do 'requires' a degree to do it, though there must be alternative ways of developing these skills. The degree, like it or not, is the screening method used by large numbers of employers and as such opens certain doors. It's certainly harder to get into all sorts of careers without a degree. The debates about university education typically revolve around routes into employment, yet for many the degree is barely relevant to the work we end up doing later on. It gives access to a certain type of career but the actual degree can often be of little practical value.

C   Lydia

There is a lot of pressure on teenagers to know exactly what they want to do with their lives. As a high-achieving student at school, the alternatives to university didn't really appeal to me. So I took up a place at a good university but ended up studying something I wasn't sure I was interested in. Some people know what they want to do from a young age, and for those people, going to university straight out of school may be a great idea. However, many of us are very unsure of our future ambitions aged 18, and should therefore be given as many choices as possible, rather than being pushed into a degree course. Many of my friends went to university straight from school.

D   Bethany

I don't really remember making the decision to go to university. Everyone always assumed I would, even though I was never the most gifted academically. Someone asked me during my second year why I had gone, and I remember not being able to answer the question. Maybe it was the way I was raised? Maybe it was the school I went to? But university was the next step. I had a great time there, I must say. It's so much more than the place you go to get a degree. You learn so many life skills that I would urge anyone to give the idea some thought. Since graduation I've had a string of jobs. University is an excellent decision for some, and may provide the right qualifications to start a career. But for others, going straight into a job is just as appropriate.

WRITING (1 hour 20 minutes)

Part 1

You **must** answer this question. Write your answer in **140–190** words in an appropriate style on the separate answer sheet.

---

1   In your English class you have been talking about life in the past. Now, your English teacher has asked you to write an essay.

Write an essay using **all** the notes and give reasons for your point of view.

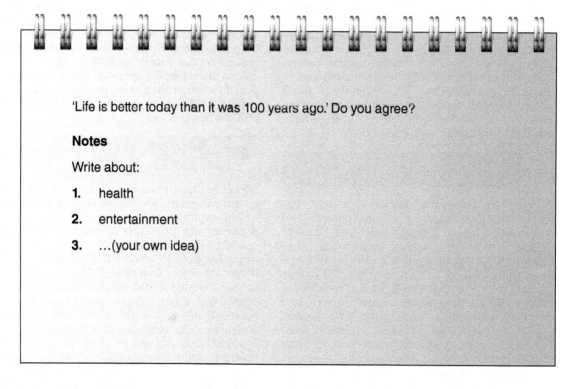

'Life is better today than it was 100 years ago.' Do you agree?

Notes

Write about:

1.   health

2.   entertainment

3.   …(your own idea)

Write your **essay**. You must use grammatically correct sentences with accurate spelling and punctuation in a style appropriate for the situation.

Part 2

Write an answer to **one** of the questions **2–4** in this part. Write your answer in **140–190** words in an appropriate style on the separate answer sheet. Put the question number in the box at the top of the answer sheet.

2   You recently saw this notice on an English-language website called TV Gold:

> **Reviews wanted!**
>
> ### A TV documentary I learnt a lot from.
>
> Have you seen an interesting TV documentary recently that you learnt a lot from? Write us a review of the documentary. You should explain what the documentary was about, tell us what you learnt from it and say whether other people would find it interesting too.
>
> The best reviews will be posted on the website next month.

Write your **review**.

3   You see this announcement on an English-language travel website.

> **ARTICLES WANTED**
>
> ## A day in the city!
>
> We are looking for articles about how a visitor could have a great time in a city in your country in just one day.
>
> Write us an article telling us what a visitor can do, what they can see and how they can travel around.
>
> The best articles will be posted on our website.

Write your **article**.

4   Your English teacher has asked you to write a report on a part-time or holiday job that you have done. The report will appear in the college English-language magazine.

In your report, you should

- describe the job
- explain what you learnt from it
- say whether you would recommend other students to do it.

Write your **report**.

LISTENING (approximately 40 minutes)

Part 1

You will hear people talking in eight different situations. For questions **1–8**, choose the best answer (**A**, **B** or **C**).

---

1   You hear a woman talking on her mobile phone about a missing piece of furniture.
How does she feel?

A   irritated with the removals company

B   unsure what's happened

C   anxious to find it quickly

2   You hear two students talking about their current course topic.
What do they agree about?

A   how boring it is

B   how difficult it is

C   how relevant it is

3   You hear two business people talking about a contract.
How does the man feel now?

A   frustrated because of the time wasted

B   surprised about the cancellation of the contract

C   sympathetic towards the other company's problems

4   You hear an artist telling a friend about an art prize he's just won.
What is he doing?

A   expressing surprise

B   admitting that he's excited

C   explaining why he thinks he was chosen

5   You overhear a women talking to a friend on her mobile phone.
Why is she phoning?

A   to explain a delay

B   to change some plans

C   to make an arrangement

6   You hear a guitarist talking about his profession.
What is the purpose of his talk?

A   to warn about the challenges of becoming a musician

B   to give step-by-step guidance on setting up a band

C   to emphasise the importance of having loyal fans

7   You hear a woman talking to a sales assistant.
Why can't she have a refund for her trainers?

A   The receipt is wrong.

B   She is not in the right shop.

C   The trainers are no longer new.

8   You hear a woman talking about a radio chat show.
What does she like about the show?

A   The presenter makes her laugh.

B   Information is given in an interesting way.

C   Guests reveal quite a lot about themselves.

Part 2

You will hear a photographer called Ian Gerrard talking about his career. For questions **9–18**, complete the sentences with a word or short phrase.

Ian Gerrard – Photographer

The subject that Ian studied at university was [_____ 9]

Ian did a presentation on [_____ 10] as part of his final year.

Ian worked for a [_____ 11] in the USA for a year after leaving

university.

When he travelled around the USA, Ian chose [_____ 12] as the

theme for his photographs.

Ian says that [_____ 13] is the season when he takes the

best photographs.

When Ian came back to Britain, he travelled around by [_____ 14]

taking photographs.

Ian says he was surprised by how few photographers specialise in shots of

[_____ 15] communities.

Ian's book will be available in bookshops in [_____ 16] next year.

The title of Ian's book is ' [_____ 17] '

Ian has chosen [_____ 18] as the theme for his next tour.

Part 3

You will hear five short extracts in which people are talking about the benefits of learning another language. For questions **19–23**, choose which benefit (**A–H**) each speaker has experienced. Use the letters only once. There are three extra letters which you do not need to use.

A   It has boosted my intellectual abilities.

B   It has improved my chances in education.

Speaker 1 ☐ **19**

C   It has made me sensitive to global issues.

Speaker 2 ☐ **20**

D   It has allowed me to gain faster promotion.

Speaker 3 ☐ **21**

E   It has made getting around in other countries easier.

Speaker 4 ☐ **22**

F   It has allowed me to help other people.

Speaker 5 ☐ **23**

G   It has advanced my awareness of the way language works.

H   It has helped me make friends.

Part 4

You will hear an interview with a woman called Patricia Jones, who is a naturalist. For questions **24–30**, choose the best answer (**A**, **B** or **C**).

24   Looking back at her work, Patricia feels

    A   surprised that her projects still attract volunteers.

    B   proud of the wide influence she's had.

    C   pleased by how she's regarded in Africa.

25   How does Patricia spend her time nowadays?

    A   persuading people to alter their behaviour

    B   advising governments on conservation

    C   studying wildlife in its natural habitat

26   How does Patricia feel about zoos?

    A   They all ought to be closed down.

    B   They should have an educational purpose.

    C   They still have a role to play in conservation.

27   In her new book, Patricia hopes to give

    A   encouragement to young scientists.

    B   advice on helping endangered animals.

    C   guidance to other environmentalists.

28   Patricia believes that children should spend time in the natural world because

    A   it is the only way to find out about it.

    B   it is essential for their development.

    C   it is a chance to change their view of animals.

29 The organisation called *In Touch* encourages young people to

    A be tolerant of each other.

    B actively work for change.

    C talk about their problems.

30 What does Patricia particularly want to do next?

    A to help girls who want to be scientists

    B to get scientists to be more responsible

    C to change people's attitudes to science

SPEAKING (14 minutes)

You take the Speaking test with another candidate (possibly two candidates), referred to here as your partner. There are two examiners. One will speak to you and your partner and the other will be listening. Both examiners will award marks.

Part 1 (2 minutes)

The examiner asks you and your partner questions about yourselves. You may be asked about things like 'your home town', 'your interests', 'your career plans', etc.

Part 2 (a one-minute 'long turn' for each candidate, plus a 30-second response from the second candidate)

The examiner gives you two photographs and asks you to talk about them for one minute. The examiner then asks your partner a question about your photographs and your partner responds briefly.

Then the examiner gives your partner two different photographs. Your partner talks about these photographs for one minute. This time the examiner asks you a question about your partner's photographs and you respond briefly.

Part 3 (4 minutes)

The examiner asks you and your partner to talk together. You may be asked to solve a problem or try to come to a decision about something. For example, you might be asked to decide the best way to use some rooms in a language school. The examiner gives you some text to help you but does not join in the conversation.

Part 4 (4 minutes)

The examiner asks some further questions, which leads to a more general discussion of what you have talked about in Part 3. You may comment on your partner's answers if you wish.

Test 2

READING AND USE OF ENGLISH (1 hour 15 minutes)

Part 1

For questions **1–8**, read the text below and decide which answer (**A, B, C** or **D**) best fits each gap. There is an example at the beginning (**0**).

Mark your answers **on the separate answer sheet**.

Example:

0   **A** predictable   **B** steady   **C** respectable   **D** main

0	A	B	C	D
	—	⊔	⊔	⊔

Home and abroad

After a short time living in a foreign country, I noticed conversations with locals assumed a **(0)** ……… pattern. There were standard answers to the usual questions. Most questions caused little **(1)** ……… – it was rather like dancing, where both partners know how to avoid **(2)** ……… on each other's toes.

But, 'When are you going home?' was a question I **(3)** ……… to answer, whenever I **(4)** ……… my life and the direction it seemed to be **(5)** ……… . In the last ten years, I had lived in a dozen countries. And I had travelled through dozens more; usually in **(6)** ……… of a purpose or a person; occasionally to see the attractions.

This kind of travel is not **(7)** ……… wandering, but is the extensive exploration of a wide **(8)** ……… of cultures. However, it doesn't allow you to put down roots. At the back of your mind, though, is the idea of home, the place you came from.

1	**A** puzzle	**B** trouble	**C** obstacle	**D** barrier
2	**A** touching	**B** moving	**C** walking	**D** stepping
3	**A** worked	**B** competed	**C** stretched	**D** struggled
4	**A** considered	**B** thought	**C** reflected	**D** believed
5	**A** making	**B** finding	**C** seeking	**D** taking
6	**A** look	**B** search	**C** sight	**D** inquiry
7	**A** aimless	**B** unreasonable	**C** unreliable	**D** indefinite
8	**A** difference	**B** arrangement	**C** variety	**D** order

Part 2

For questions **9–16**, read the text below and think of the word which best fits each gap. Use only **one** word in each gap. There is an example at the beginning (**0**).

Write your answers **IN CAPITAL LETTERS on the separate answer sheet**.

Example: | 0 | | U | P | | | | | | | | | | | | | | | | |

An Irish cookery school

In the last few years, a number of cookery schools have been set **(0)** ……… in Ireland to promote Irish cooking. **(9)** ……… such school is run by Kathleen Doyle not **(10)** ……… from the centre of Dublin.

'I opened the school twelve years ago,' says Kathleen. 'The school was by no means an overnight success; I found **(11)** ……… necessary to work hard to build up a reputation. One of my advantages was that I'd had problems with my own cooking. I've made **(12)** ……… mistake that it's possible to make, but **(13)** ……… of this, I know what people do wrong from first-hand experience.'

Just **(14)** ……… most cookery schools in Ireland, Kathleen initially copied the classical dishes of France and Italy and other countries **(15)** ……… have a reputation for excellent food. 'Now though, things are changing,' says Kathleen. 'We get excellent produce from Irish farms and, **(16)** ……… a result, we're encouraging students to create unique Irish dishes.'

Part 3

For questions **17–24**, read the text below. Use the word given in capitals at the end of some of the lines to form a word that fits in the gap **in the same line**. There is an example at the beginning (**0**).

Write your answers **IN CAPITAL LETTERS on the separate answer sheet**.

Example:

| 0 | C | O | M | P | E | T | I | T | O | R | S | | | | | | |

Running speed

Elite **(0)** .... like the Jamaican Usain Bolt have regularly been clocked   **COMPETE**

running at nearly 45 kilometres per hour. Such speed would have seemed

(17) .... not so long ago. Scientists now suggest that humans can   **BELIEVE**

move **(18)** .... faster than even that, perhaps as fast as 65 kilometres   **CONSIDER**

per hour.

For years, it was assumed that simple muscle power determined human

speed, but recent research suggests otherwise. The most important

(19) .... factor appears to be how quickly the muscles can contract   **LIMIT**

and thus **(20)** .... the time a runner's foot is in contact with the ground.   **MINIMUM**

Is our athletic ability inherited? Researcher Alun Williams has **(21)** ....   **IDENTITY**

twenty-three inherited factors that influence sporting performance, such

as the **(22)** .... use of oxygen, and strength. As world population rises,   **EFFICIENCY**

predicts Williams, the **(23)** .... of there being someone with the right   **POSSIBLE**

genes for these twenty-three **(24)** .... will increase noticeably and thus   **CHARACTER**

faster runners are likely to emerge in future.

Part 4

For questions **25–30**, complete the second sentence so that it has a similar meaning to the first sentence, using the word given. **Do not change the word given.** You must use between **two** and **five** words, including the word given. Here is an example (**0**).

Example:

0   A very friendly taxi driver drove us into town.

   DRIVEN

   We .... a very friendly taxi driver.

The gap can be filled by the words 'were driven into town by', so you write:

Example: | **0** | *WERE DRIVEN INTO TOWN BY* |

Write **only** the missing words **IN CAPITAL LETTERS on the separate answer sheet.**

---

25   Robert had never been to Turkey on business before.

   FIRST

   It .... Robert had ever been to Turkey on business.

26   It was impossible for me to know which road to follow.

   NOT

   I .... known which road to follow.

27   So far this year the cost of petrol has not increased.

   INCREASE

   So far this year there .... in the cost of petrol.

28 I cannot get all my clothes in the suitcase.

BIG

The suitcase ……………………………………………… take all my clothes.

29 The waiter carried the tray very carefully so that he wouldn't spill any of the drinks.

AVOID

The waiter carried the tray very carefully so ……………………………………………… any of the drinks.

30 I wasn't able to get to the airport on time because of the bad weather.

PREVENTED

The bad weather ……………………………………………… to the airport on time.

Part 5

You are going to read an article about an island off the west coast of Scotland. For questions **31–36**, choose the answer (**A**, **B**, **C** or **D**) which you think fits best according to the text.

Mark your answers **on the separate answer sheet**.

The Isle of Muck

Jim Richardson visits the Scottish island of Muck.

Lawrence MacEwen crouches down on his Scottish island, the Isle of Muck. And so do I. An Atlantic gale threatens to lift and blow us both out like October leaves, over the steep cliff at our feet and across the bay 120 m below, dropping us in the surrounding ocean. Then MacEwen's sheepdog, Tie, creeps up and his blond, bearded owner strokes him with gentle hands. The howling wind, rage as it might, can't make this man uncomfortable here, on his island, where he looks – and is – perfectly at home.

MacEwen is giving me a visual tour of his neighbourhood. Nodding to the north, he yells, 'That island is Eigg. The one to the west of it is the Isle of Rum. It gets twice as much rain as we do.' I watch heavy clouds dump rain on its huge mountains. 'Just beyond Rum is the island of Soay.' 'I have sheep to move,' MacEwen abruptly announces when rain drifts towards us. We start down the slopes. As we stride along, he brings me up to speed on island details: Volcanic Muck is 3 km long and half as wide; its geese eat vast amounts of grass; and the MacEwens have been living here for 3,000 years.

Herding the sheep interrupts the flow of information. Tie, the sheepdog, is circling a flock of sheep – and not doing it well. 'Away to me, Tie. *Away to me*,' meaning the dog should circle to the right. He doesn't; he goes straight up the middle of the flock, creating confusion. 'Tie.' MacEwen's voice drips disappointment. 'That will never do.' The dog looks ashamed.

The Isle of Muck is largely a MacEwen enterprise. Lawrence runs the farm with his wife, Jenny; son Colin, newly married, manages the island cottages; and daughter Mary runs the island hotel, Port Mor, with her husband, Toby. Mary and Toby love the fact that their two boys can wander the island on their own and sail dinghies on summer days. 'They go out of the door and come back only when they're hungry.' But island life has its compromises. For one, electricity is only available part of the time. My first evening, I wait anxiously for the lights to turn on. The next morning I find Mary setting out breakfast by torchlight. But I cope with it – along with no mobile phone service. 'There is mobile reception on the hill,' Mary tells me. 'Most visitors try for a couple of days, then just put the phone in the drawer.' So I do too.

Everything on Muck seems delightfully improbable. The boat today brings over the post – and three musicians, who hop off carrying instruments. Their concert in the island's tearoom proves a smash hit, with the islanders present tapping their boots in time to the music. That night, sitting by a glowing fire as it rains outside, Lawrence MacEwen tells me how he met his wife, Jenny. 'Her father saw a small farm on the isle of Soay advertised in the newspaper, and bought it without even looking at it. He'd never been to Scotland. Jenny was sent to manage it.' Did Jenny know anything about running a farm? 'She had good typing skills.'

I go to bed with rain and awake to more rain. But I eat well, virtually every bit of food coming from the tiny island. Mary sends me down to fisherman Sandy Mathers for fresh fish. I carry it back through the village and deliver it to Mary at the kitchen door. By 7 pm, our fish is on the table, delicious beyond reckoning. Also beyond reckoning: my ferry ride the following morning to my next island. Over the preceding two months, many of the scheduled ferries had been cancelled because of high seas. If my ferry didn't come, I'd be stuck on Muck for two more days. Which, now, phone or no phone, was *line 7.* what I secretly longed for.

31 Why does the writer describe MacEwen stroking his dog?

    A to emphasise how bad MacEwen thought the weather was that day
    B to show the dog was as frightened by the storm as MacEwan was
    C to explain why MacEwen had risked going to the dangerous cliffs
    D to demonstrate how relaxed MacEwen was despite the bad weather

32 According to the writer, the sheepdog's behaviour suggests that

    A it never obeys MacEwen.
    B it is afraid of MacEwen.
    C it is aware it should have done better.
    D it usually responds to loud commands.

33 What is suggested about island life in the fourth paragraph?

    A People living there would like more visitors to help the economy.
    B People come to the island in search of employment.
    C People are too busy to do all the things they'd like to.
    D People don't mind putting up with some inconveniences.

34 What attitude is expressed by the writer in the fifth paragraph?

    A He is amused that people on the island share their feelings so openly.
    B He likes the way so many surprising things can happen on the island.
    C He approves of the way the islanders all socialise together.
    D He finds it strange that island farms are advertised in national newspapers.

35 What does 'Which' refer to in line 75?

    A the writer's ferry ride
    B the next island
    C having to stay on the island
    D a mobile phone

36 From the text as a whole, we find out the island of Muck

    A is a safe place for children to live.
    B has the highest level of rainfall in the area.
    C has an economy based solely on sheep.
    D is dependent on the outside world for its food.

Part 6

You are going to read a newspaper article about the Hollywood sign in the United States of America. Six sentences have been removed from the article. Choose from the sentences **A–H** the one which fits each gap (**37–42**). There is one extra sentence which you do not need to use.

Mark your answers **on the separate answer sheet**.

The sign on a hill

At the top of a hill called Mount Lee in Los Angeles on the west coast of the USA is a very famous sign, recognisable to people around the world. My job is to look after this sign. It says *Hollywood* and that's of course the place where films have been made for over a hundred years. The first film was made there in 1907 and by 1912, at least 15 independent studios could be found making films around town.

The film industry continued to grow and the name Hollywood, which by the 1920s represented not just a city but also an industry and a lifestyle, was made official when the 'Hollywoodland' sign was erected in 1923. It was only supposed to last about a year. **37** But it wasn't always. It started out as a massive billboard advertising an upscale suburban development called Hollywoodland.

In the 1940s, TV started to become popular and some Hollywood film studios closed, but then TV companies moved in and took them over. At this point, the city of Los Angeles decided to renovate the sign. The letters spelling 'land' were removed and the rest was repaired. Modern Hollywood was born. The letters in the sign weren't straight and still aren't. **38** They follow the shape of Mount Lee and this is part of their fame.

I am responsible for maintaining and protecting the sign. **39** When I first arrived in 1989, security was pretty low-tech – we put up a fence around the sign to stop trespassers messing with it. But people just jumped over the fence. The back of the sign was black with graffiti – there was barbed wire across it, but they still got through. So I decided to improve the effectiveness of the security.

Now we have motion-detectors and cameras. Everything goes via the internet to a dedicated surveillance team watching various structures around the city. **40** But they can get a closer look on one of my regular tours.

It's also important to protect the sign's image as it's used in loads of adverts and news pieces. There's a simple rule about how the sign can be used. **41** However, it mostly comes down to the look. To take a different example, if you used 'Hollywood' in the name of your company it would depend what the word looked like, whether it was just spelled out or whether the image of the sign itself was used.

People call up with the most ridiculous ideas. They want to light the sign, paint it pink, or cover it in something to promote their product. You'll get a really enthusiastic marketing executive call up, terribly excited because they think they're the first person to think of this or that idea. **42** That's because we don't like to change the image and we hope it will have the same significance for generations to come.

A Even so, people still try to climb over the barrier, mostly innocent tourists surprised that you can't walk right up to the sign.

B They mostly get turned down.

C If one of them ever fell down I would have to put it back up at exactly the same angle.

D We used to have real problems.

E Things have changed a lot since then.

F It's still there, of course, and is a symbol of the entertainment world.

G If the purpose is commercial – to promote something – payment has to be made.

Part 7

You are going to read an article in which four athletes talk about what they eat. For questions **43–52**, choose from the athletes (**A–D**). The athletes may be chosen more than once.

Mark your answers **on the separate answer sheet**.

Which athlete

enjoys cooking but finds the planning difficult?	**43**	
has to carry food with him when training?	**44**	
doesn't find it easy to eat before an event?	**45**	
uses cooking as a way to relax?	**46**	
sometimes allows himself certain food as a reward?	**47**	
has seen a change in the diet of sports people?	**48**	
once made the wrong decision about the food he ate?	**49**	
says that people are unaware of what he actually eats?	**50**	
says knowing what and when to eat is critical?	**51**	
has had to change his diet with a change of sport?	**52**	

Sports diets

Four athletes talk about what they eat.

A Mark

When I'm cycling on my own I stuff my pockets with bananas and protein bars. On the longest rides I'll eat something every half an hour. For heavier training it's physically impossible to get enough energy from food alone, so you do rely on energy drinks. One development in sports nutrition since I've been competing is the focus on the importance of protein. Cycling is much more weight-orientated than the swimming I used to do, which means I need to eat differently now. Protein feeds the muscles but keeps them as lean as possible. I've been an athlete for 20 years so healthy eating is normal for me, but that's not to say I don't get a tasty take-away meal from time to time. I've just learned to spot the meals that will provide what I need. It's simple things like steering clear of the creamy sauces and making sure I get lots of veg.

B Stefan

Everyone says: 'As a runner you must be on a really strict diet. Do you only eat salad? Are you allowed chocolate?' But that's really not the case. I've got salad and vegetables in my shopping trolley but there's always some chocolate in there, too. I do most of the cooking at home. On the morning of a competition, I get so nervous I feel really sick. I have to force myself to have something so I'll have enough energy to perform well. Sometimes I get those days where I don't want to be so disciplined. You think: 'I've trained really hard, I deserve to have a pizza.' It's OK to have a little relapse every now and then but I can't do it every day or I'd be rolling round the track!

C Guy

For a gymnast, a kilo can make all the difference. But if you don't eat enough you'll be a bit shaky and weak. It's all about eating the right amount, at the right time – two hours before you do anything. Breakfast is fruit and if I'm a bit peckish, wholewheat toast and butter! I get to training for 12 pm, then break after three hours for lunch – more fruit, a cheese and tomato sandwich. I'm back in the gym from 5 pm to 8 pm, then I go to my Mum's for steak and vegetables or chicken and salad. I don't tend to mix carbs with meat late at night. I'm not the best cook, but I think it's fun to do. I know how to make chicken from my mum's recipe, it just takes me a bit longer to get organised.

D Tomas

It's definitely possible to eat delicious food and be a professional swimmer. I've always loved food so I'm not going to be obsessive because you can get what you need and still enjoy every bite. I'm not really one for endless protein shakes and energy drinks. Before a training session I'd rather have a banana. That's not to say I'm perfect. At the world championships I got my feeding strategy wrong – and I paid for it. For my sport it's what you eat two days before the competition that makes the difference. You have to 'carb load' – eat piles of rice or pasta – and I didn't. I was leading for a long way but I ended up 11th. My biggest indulgence is pastry. And I love baking. I train for 33 hours a week so in my time off I need to rest, and spending time in the kitchen is perfect. Swimming is my biggest passion but baking comes a close second.

(1 hour 20 minutes)

Part 1

You **must** answer this question. Write your answer in **140–190** words in an appropriate style **on the separate answer sheet**.

---

1   In your English class you have been talking about relationships. Now, your English teacher has asked you to write an essay.

Write an essay using **all** the notes and give reasons for your point of view.

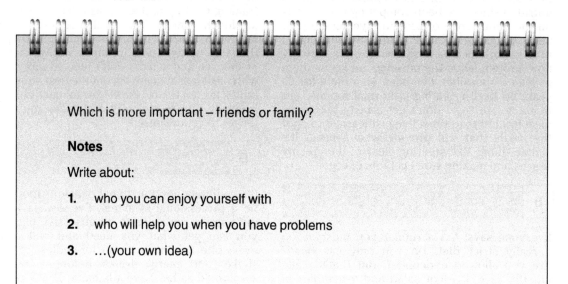

Which is more important – friends or family?

Notes

Write about:

1.   who you can enjoy yourself with

2.   who will help you when you have problems

3.   …(your own idea)

Write your **essay**. You must use grammatically correct sentences with accurate spelling and punctuation in a style appropriate for the situation.

Part 2

Write an answer to **one** of the questions 2–4 in this part. Write your answer in **140–190** words in an appropriate style **on the separate answer sheet**. Put the question number in the box at the top of the answer sheet.

---

2   You recently saw this notice on an English-language website called Book World.

> **Reviews wanted!**
>
> ### The best thriller I have ever read!
>
> Have you read a thriller recently that you think other readers would enjoy?
> Write us a review of the book. You should include information on:
>
> - what it's about
> - why it's exciting
> - who you would recommend it to.
>
> The best reviews will be posted on the website next month.

Write your **review**.

3   You see this announcement on an English-language website.

Write your **article**.

> **ARTICLES WANTED**
>
> # The most interesting weekend of my life
>
> Write us an article about the most interesting weekend of your life. Explain what happened and where, and why it was so interesting.
>
> The best articles will be posted on our website.

4   You have received this email from your English-speaking friend, Kim.

> It's really kind of you to let me stay at your flat while you're on holiday. Please could you let me know how to get the keys? And could you also tell me anything else I need to know about the flat and whether there's anywhere near that I can buy food?
>
> Thanks, Kim

Write your **email**.

LISTENING (approximately 40 minutes)

Part 1

You will hear people talking in eight different situations. For questions **1–8**, choose the best answer (**A**, **B** or **C**).

---

1   You hear a man talking about how his business became successful.
Where did his additional funding come from?

   A   the local bank

   B   a family friend

   C   his own savings

2   You hear a woman talking about a journey.
How did she travel?

   A   by boat

   B   by train

   C   by coach

3   You overhear a man talking to his wife on the phone.
What is he talking about?

   A   buying a car

   B   booking a holiday

   C   moving abroad

4   You hear two students talking about their course.
What does the woman think about the course?

   A   It is quite difficult.

   B   It is worth doing.

   C   It is becoming more interesting.

5 You hear a woman talking about roller derby, a hobby which involves speed racing on skates. What is she doing?

A explaining what made her decide to take it up

B appreciating her friends' attitude to the sport

C describing how she feels when she's taking part

6 You hear part of a radio programme. What is the woman talking about?

A a new shop

B a new exhibition

C a new leisure centre

7 You overhear two students discussing a reading project they did with young children. What do they agree about it?

A The venue was perfect.

B The material was well received.

C The number of participants was surprising.

8 You hear an actor talking about the character she plays in a TV drama series. How does she feel about the character?

A She is envious of her life-style.

B She sympathises with her current problems.

C She admires her intelligence.

Part 2

You will hear a woman called Gina Purvis, who is a pilot for a commercial airline, talking about her job. For questions **9–18**, complete the sentences with a word or short phrase.

Sky high

Gina disliked her first job as a [_____ **9**] .

The airline that Gina works for insists on at least [_____ **10**]

hours of flying experience from their captains.

Gina says that because her husband is a [_____ **11**] he is

tolerant of her job.

The 'Notices to Pilots' provides information about any [_____ **12**]

that are experiencing problems.

Gina says that if she has extra [_____ **13**] she will need more fuel

for her flight.

Gina explains that many pilots she works with did a degree in

[_____ **14**] at university.

Gina says that all the [_____ **15**] must be within reach of the two

pilots in the cockpit.

The pilots look at a [_____ **16**] to check if anyone is standing

at the cockpit entrance.

Gina gets information from a [_____ **17**] about any small

problems on the plane.

Gina says what she really appreciates is a [_____ **18**] flight.

Part 3

You will hear five short extracts in which students are talking about a trip they have taken. For questions **19–23**, choose from the list (**A–H**) what each student says about their trip. Use the letters only once. There are three extra letters which you do not need to use.

A   Someone I met while I was there is coming to visit me soon.

B   I plan to do things a little differently on my next visit.

Speaker 1		19

C   I learnt more about some friends while I was with them.

Speaker 2		20

D   I enjoyed myself thanks to one person's efforts.

Speaker 3		21

E   My experience was different when I returned to a place.

Speaker 4		22

F   Some people there offered to take me on a tour.

Speaker 5		23

G   I didn't take to the city at first.

H   I went back to a place I had never expected to see again.

Part 4

You will hear an interview with a musician called Jarrold Harding, who's talking about his career. For questions **24–30**, choose the best answer (**A**, **B** or **C**).

24 How did Jarrold's interest in music begin?

    A He went to one of his father's concerts.

    B He was given lessons by an orchestra violinist.

    C He watched musicians practising.

25 Jarrold played in his first concert

    A together with his mother.

    B when he was away on holiday with his parents.

    C to make his father happy.

26 What impressed Jarrold about his mother's musical ability?

    A She never made any mistakes.

    B She could memorise music very quickly.

    C She could adapt piano music for his violin.

27 What does Jarrold say about his interest in conducting?

    A It began at an early age.

    B It was encouraged by his father.

    C It increased when he heard famous musicians.

28 How did Jarrold feel when he was at college?

    A relieved to find he didn't have to work too hard

    B pleased at how well he played compared to everyone else

    C glad he could cope with things that some students struggled with

29 What did Jarrold do after leaving college?

    A He tried to devote all his time to conducting.

    B He was introduced to a good conducting teacher.

    C He had lessons with a famous conductor.

30 Jarrold thinks that being both a violinist and a conductor

    A has given him opportunities to develop as a musician.

    B has allowed him more freedom to play where he wants.

    C has earned him the respect of other professionals.

SPEAKING (14 minutes)

You take the Speaking test with another candidate (possibly two candidates), referred to here as your partner. There are two examiners. One will speak to you and your partner and the other will be listening. Both examiners will award marks.

Part 1 (2 minutes)

The examiner asks you and your partner questions about yourselves. You may be asked about things like 'your home town', 'your interests', 'your career plans', etc.

Part 2 (a one-minute 'long turn' for each candidate, plus a 30-second response from the second candidate)

The examiner gives you two photographs and asks you to talk about them for one minute. The examiner then asks your partner a question about your photographs and your partner responds briefly.

Then the examiner gives your partner two different photographs. Your partner talks about these photographs for one minute. This time the examiner asks you a question about your partner's photographs and you respond briefly.

Part 3 (4 minutes)

The examiner asks you and your partner to talk together. You may be asked to solve a problem or try to come to a decision about something. For example, you might be asked to decide the best way to use some rooms in a language school. The examiner gives you some text to help you but does not join in the conversation.

Part 4 (4 minutes)

The examiner asks some further questions, which leads to a more general discussion of what you have talked about in Part 3. You may comment on your partner's answers if you wish.

Test 3

READING AND USE OF ENGLISH (1 hour 15 minutes)

Part 1

For questions **1–8**, read the text below and decide which answer (**A, B, C** or **D**) best fits each gap. There is an example at the beginning (**0**).

Mark your answers **on the separate answer sheet**.

Example:

0 **A** inviting   **B** attracting   **C** involving   **D** appealing

0	A	B	C	D
	▬	▭	▭	▭

New words for a dictionary

The editors of a new online dictionary are **(0)** .... the public to submit words that they would like to see in the dictionary. People are already sending in words, some of which they have **(1)** .... themselves – these will almost certainly not **(2)** .... in the dictionary!

When a new word is submitted, editors check newspapers, radio, television and social networks to see how **(3)** .... the word is used. They also **(4)** .... whether the word is likely to remain in use for more than one or two years. The evidence they collect will help them decide whether or not to put it in the dictionary.

Editors will **(5)** .... feedback on any words submitted by the public. Even words not accepted will **(6)** .... to be monitored over the following year. Editors need to be **(7)** .... of new words which emerge from areas such as popular culture and technology, so that their dictionary is a genuine **(8)** .... of the current language.

1	**A** set out	**B** made up	**C** brought out	**D** come up
2	**A** include	**B** show	**C** consist	**D** appear
3	**A** totally	**B** widely	**C** fully	**D** vastly
4	**A** consider	**B** regard	**C** prove	**D** rate
5	**A** state	**B** tell	**C** provide	**D** inform
6	**A** keep	**B** rest	**C** last	**D** continue
7	**A** familiar	**B** aware	**C** alert	**D** experience
8	**A** mark	**B** copy	**C** reflection	**D** imitation

Part 2

For questions **9–16**, read the text below and think of the word which best fits each gap. Use only **one** word in each gap. There is an example at the beginning (**0**).

Write your answers **IN CAPITAL LETTERS on the separate answer sheet**.

Example: | **0** | *I* | *S* | | | | | | | | | | | | | | | | | |

Animal communication

It (**0**) .... sometimes said that animals use language. Certainly some animal species have developed amazingly sophisticated ways of communicating with (**9**) .... another.

But there are huge differences between the ways animals communicate and the ways human beings do. When animals make a sound, such (**10**) .... a bark or a call, it is in reaction to (**11**) .... is happening around them. An alarm call means they are frightened. A hunger call means they want food. Animals, though, cannot make a call meaning 'I was scared yesterday' or 'I'll be hungry tomorrow'. Only human beings are capable (**12**) .... doing this.

Zoologists have had some success in teaching human language to animals. (**13**) .... some famous experiments, chimpanzees have (**14**) .... taught to use their hands to give information on a range of things. Some animals have even managed to put signs together in (**15**) .... to make simple sentences. However, getting them to do this takes a huge (**16**) .... of training.

Part 3

For questions **17–24**, read the text below. Use the word given in capitals at the end of some of the lines to form a word that fits in the gap **in the same line**. There is an example at the beginning **(0)**.

Write your answers **IN CAPITAL LETTERS on the separate answer sheet**.

Example:

0	C	Y	C	L	I	S	T											

Cycling

I have been a keen **(0)** ………. for about nine years. When I began cycling,   **CYCLE**

I found the flat roads easy but the hills almost **(17)** ……….. . Surprisingly,   **POSSIBLE**

now it's the opposite. A long flat ride can be both dull and **(18)** ………..   **EXHAUST**

as you never experience that fantastic feeling of freedom when speeding

downhill. Years ago, going uphill left me **(19)** ……….. . Now I have learned   **BREATH**

to take hills slowly and steadily.

When I set off, I'm full of energy and the first hundred metres are

(20) ……….., the next couple of kilometres a bit tiring, but on the whole the   **MARVEL**

experience is very **(21)** ……….. .   **ENJOY**

Cycling is **(22)** ……….. any other forms of exercise I have tried; it is never   **LIKE**

a chore but always a **(23)** ……….. . The physical benefits are obvious but   **PLEASE**

the mental benefits are **(24)** ……….. important; when you are travelling   **EQUAL**

calmly at a sensible speed, you breathe fresh air, have time to think and

can relax.

Part 4

For questions **25–30**, complete the second sentence so that it has a similar meaning to the first sentence, using the word given. **Do not change the word given.** You must use between **two** and **five** words, including the word given. Here is an example (**0**).

Example:

0   A very friendly taxi driver drove us into town.

   DRIVEN

   We .... a very friendly taxi driver.

The gap can be filled by the words 'were driven into town by', so you write:

Example:	0	*WERE DRIVEN INTO TOWN BY*

Write **only** the missing words **IN CAPITAL LETTERS on the separate answer sheet**.

---

25   My brother doesn't play tennis now as well as he used to.

   BETTER

   My brother used to .... does now.

26   Clothing companies are selling an increasing number of goods on the internet.

   BOUGHT

   An increasing number of goods .... clothing companies on the internet.

27   'Well done for scoring twice, Mark,' said the coach.

   PRAISED

   Mark .... for scoring twice.

28 You are welcome to contact me if you need more information.

TOUCH

Please feel free .... me if you need more information.

29 Tickets for the concert cannot be bought before 12th May.

SALE

Tickets for the concert will not .... 12th May.

30 I didn't buy the camera because it was so expensive.

BEEN

I would have bought the camera .... so expensive.

Part 5

You are going to read part of an autobiography in which a gardener talks about his childhood and his love of plants and the countryside. For questions **31–36**, choose the answer (**A**, **B**, **C** or **D**) which you think fits best according to the text.

Mark your answers **on the separate answer sheet**.

Green fingers

It never occurred to me when I was little that gardens were anything less than glamorous places. Grandad's garden was on the bank of a river and sloped gently down towards the water. You couldn't reach the river but you could hear the sound of the water and the birds that sang in the trees above. I imagined that all gardens were like this – a place of escape, peace and solitude. Grandad's plot was nothing out of the ordinary when it came to features. He had nothing as grand as a greenhouse, unlike some of his neighbours. Not that they had proper 'bought' greenhouses. Theirs were made from old window frames. Patches of plastic would be tacked in place where a carelessly wielded spade had smashed a pane of glass.

At home, his son, my father, could be quiet and withdrawn. I wouldn't want to make him sound humourless. He wasn't. Silly things would amuse him. He had phrases that he liked to use, 'It's immaterial to me' being one of them. 'I don't mind' would have done just as well but he liked the word 'immaterial'. I realise that, deep down, he was probably disappointed that he hadn't made more of his life. He left school without qualifications and became apprenticed to a plumber. Plumbing was not something he was passionate about. It was just what he did. He was never particularly ambitious, though there was a moment when he and Mum
line 14　thought of emigrating to Canada, but it came to nothing. Where he came into his own was around the house. He had an 'eye for the job'. Be it bookshelves or a cupboard – what he could achieve was astonishing.

My parents moved house only once in their entire married life. But my mother made up for this lack of daring when it came to furniture. You would just get used to the shape of one chair when another appeared, but the most dramatic change of all was the arrival of a piano. I always wanted to like it but it did its best to intimidate me. The only thing I did like about it were the two brass candlesticks that jutted out from the front. 'They're too posh', my mother said and they disappeared one day while I was at school. There was never any mention of my being allowed to play it. Instead lessons were booked for my sister. When I asked my mother in later life why I wasn't given the opportunity, her reply was brief: 'You'd never have practised'.

Of the three options, moors, woods or river – the river was the one that usually got my vote. On a stretch of the river I was allowed to disappear with my imagination into another world. With a fishing net over my shoulder I could set off in sandals that were last year's model, with the fronts cut out to accommodate toes that were now right to the end. I'd walk along the river bank looking for a suitable spot where I could take off the painful sandals and leave them with my picnic while I ventured out, tentatively, peering through the water for any fish that I could scoop up with the net and take home. After the first disastrous attempts to keep them alive in the back yard, they were tipped back into the water.

I wanted to leave school as soon as possible but that seemed an unlikely prospect until one day my father announced, 'They've got a vacancy for an apprentice gardener in the Parks Department. I thought you might be interested.' In one brief moment Dad had gone against his better judgement. He might still have preferred it if I became a carpenter. But I like to feel that somewhere inside him was a feeling that things might just turn out for the best. If I stuck at it. Maybe I'm deceiving myself, but I prefer to believe that in his heart, although he hated gardening himself, he'd watched me doing it for long enough and noticed my unfailing passion for all things that grew and flowered and fruited.

31 When the writer describes his grandad's garden, he is

    A proud that his granddad was such a good gardener.
    B embarrassed that the garden was not as good as others nearby.
    C indignant that items in the garden were often damaged.
    D positive about the time he spent in the garden.

32 What is the writer's attitude to his father in the second paragraph?

    A regretful that his father had not achieved more
    B irritated that his father used words he didn't understand
    C sympathetic to the reasons why his father behaved as he did
    D grateful that his father had not taken the family to Canada

33 What does the writer mean by the phrase 'came into his own' in line 14?

    A was able to do something by himself
    B was able to show how talented he was
    C was able to continue his day job
    D was able to forget his failures

34 What was the writer's first reaction to the piano?

    A surprise when it suddenly appeared
    B pleasure at seeing it in the living room
    C anger that only his sister would have piano lessons
    D pride that his mother had listened to his advice

35 The writer's description of his fishing trips illustrate

    A how much free time he was given.
    B how beautiful the river was.
    C how good a fisherman he was.
    D how carefree his childhood was.

36 What is the main idea of the last paragraph?

    A His father did not want his son to be a gardener.
    B His father was tired of disagreeing with his son.
    C His father had been impressed by his son's love of gardening.
    D His father had been trying to find a job his son would enjoy.

Part 6

You are going to read an article about the experience of running while listening to music. Six sentences have been removed from the article. Choose from the sentences **A–G** the one which fits each gap (**37–42**). There is one extra sentence which you do not need to use.

Mark your answers **on the separate answer sheet**.

Does music make you run faster?

Runner Adharanand Finn took part in an unusual race in order to test the theory that music can make you run faster.

An expert on the effects of music on exercise, Dr Costas Karageorghis, claims that listening to music while running can boost performance by up to 15%. To put this theory to the test, I took part in a special Rock 'n' Roll half marathon, which had groups of musicians playing at various points along the route.

As I lined up at the start with almost 4,000 other runners, a singer sang an inspiring song for us. It may explain why I got off to a good start. I only came eighth in the end, though, even though I'd just spent six months training hard. **37** However, it turns out that all the training may have affected my response to the music; according to the research, the benefits of listening to music decrease with the level of intensity of the running.

'Elite athletes,' says Karageorghis, 'tend to focus inwardly when they are running.' According to him, most other runners look for stimulus and distraction from what is going on around them. 'Judging by your time,' he says, 'you are one of the former.' It is true. Apart from the song at the start, when I was standing still, I can barely remember the music played along the course. The first act I passed, a folk group, made me smile, and at one point I found myself running in time to the beat of some hard rock. **38** I can't say they helped my performance very much. But what did other runners make of the music?

Adam Bull usually runs marathons with no music and little crowd support. ' **39** With the upbeat bands, you find yourself running to the beat, which helps. It also brings out people to cheer you on.' Rosie Bradford was also a convert. 'As we ran past one band and they started playing *These Boots Were Made for Walking*, everybody suddenly went faster.'

The only person I found who was less than happy with the music was Lois Lloyd. 'There wasn't enough of it, and I found it wasn't loud enough, so I ran with an MP3 player.' she said. ' **40** ' Karageorghis is not surprised when I tell him. 'There are many advantages to using your own player, rather than relying on the music on the course,' he says. 'It gives you a constant stimulus, rather than just an occasional one, and you can tailor the playlist to your taste.'

One runner told me there was a direct correlation between the quality of the music on the course and how much it helped. But quality, of course, is subjective. I remember feeling annoyed as I ran past one band playing *Keep On Running*. **41**

Of course, the music was not only there to help runners break their personal bests (although sadly it was unable to help me beat mine), but to provide a sense of occasion, draw out the crowds and create a carnival atmosphere. **42** As I left, people were beginning to relax after the run, listening to an excellent rock band. It was a fitting way to end the day.

A I need my music all the time.

B I think they knew why I found the music here so distracting.

C I enjoyed that for a few moments, but both of them came and went in a flash.

D Along with some spring sunshine, it certainly achieved that.

E Someone else, though, may have found it uplifting.

F I was, in fact, taking my running pretty seriously at that time.

G The music here has been great for my performance.

Part 7

You are going to read four reviews of a science documentary series on TV. For questions **43–52**, choose from the reviews (**A–D**). The reviews may be chosen more than once.

Mark your answers **on the separate answer sheet**.

In which review does it say that

an effort was made to connect a number of unrelated issues?	43
the topics covered are well chosen?	44
viewers are shown how science can occasionally do better than nature?	45
the series deals with something people have hoped to achieve for a while?	46
the series unfortunately didn't spend a lot of time explaining the topics covered?	47
viewers are clearly informed?	48
it's good that viewers are not required to consider all aspects of the subject carefully?	49
the series was worth making despite the topic not appearing very interesting at first?	50
viewers may not always find the series comfortable to watch?	51
the series achieves its aims by astonishing its viewers?	52

Reviews of TV science documentary series

Paul Hansen looks at the latest science programmes.

A — Science for All

Fortunately for me and non-scientists everywhere, the makers of *Science for All* are there to plug the gaps in our knowledge. The series is rather like a knowledgeable parent who doesn't mind being pestered by wide-eyed and curious children: it takes the time to explain all those fascinating mysteries of nature in an entertaining and understandable way. The last series opened my eyes to all manner of interesting facts and demystified some of the problems faced by modern physics. And the new series shows no lack of inspiration for subjects to tackle: everything from the existence of life on other planets to the odd properties of human memory are rightly considered suitable subjects. So, while it's a shame that factual programmes are getting increasingly scarce these days, it's a comfort that *Science for All* shows no signs of dipping in quality or disappearing from public view.

B — Out in Space

Although I wasn't expecting much from this series, I'm pleased that the producers of *Out in Space* persisted with their unpromising subject. In the course of the first programme we learn about hurricanes, deserts, and even how the Moon was made; a bewildering mix of phenomena that, we were assured, were all caused by events beyond our planet's atmosphere. That's not to say the programme explored them in any great detail, preferring to skip breathlessly from one to the next. The essential logic of the series seemed to be that if you take any natural phenomenon and ask 'why?' enough times, the answers will eventually be that it's something to do with space. The two presenters attempted to get it all to fit together, by taking part in exciting activities. Sadly these only occasionally succeeded.

C — Stars and Planets

The second series of *Stars and Planets* is an attempt to take advantage of the success of the first, which unexpectedly gained a substantial general audience. Like its predecessor, this is big on amazing photography and fabulous graphics, most of which are much less successful at communicating the immensity of the ideas involved than one human being talking to you directly. This time the scope is even wider, astronomically speaking. What we are being introduced to here are ambitious ideas about time and space, and the presenter succeeds rather better than you might expect. It helps that he doesn't go too deep, as once you start thinking about it this is tricky stuff to get your head around. The point of such programmes is less to explain every detail than to arouse a generalised sense of amazement that might lead to further thinking, and *Stars and Planets* is certainly good at that.

D — Robot Technology

This ground-breaking science documentary series follows a group of experts as they attempt to build a complete artificial human from robotic body parts. The project sees scientists use the latest technology from the world's most renowned research centres and manufacturers. It is the realisation of a long-held dream to create a human from manufactured parts, using everything from bionic arms and mechanical hearts, eye implants and microchip brains. The series explores to what extent modern technology is capable of replacing body parts – or even improving their abilities. The presenter, very appropriately, has an artificial hand himself. This ambitious series gives us a guided tour of the wonders of modern technology. Though it can be a slightly upsetting journey at times, it engages the audience in a revolution that is changing the face of medicine.

'1 hour 20 minutes)

Part 1

You **must** answer this question. Write your answer in **140–190** words in an appropriate style **on the separate answer sheet**.

---

1   In your English class you have been talking about work. Now, your English teacher has asked you to write an essay.

Write an essay using **all** the notes and give reasons for your point of view.

Is it better to earn a lot of money or to enjoy your job?

Notes

Write about:

1.   how much time is spent at work

2.   the type of work which is done

3.   …(your own idea)

Write your **essay**. You must use grammatically correct sentences with accurate spelling and punctuation in a style appropriate for the situation.

Part 2

Write an answer to **one** of the questions **2–4** in this part. Write your answer in **140–190** words in an appropriate style **on the separate answer sheet**. Put the question number in the box at the top of the answer sheet.

---

2   Your college would like to start an English-language film club where people can go to watch films in English and discuss them. Your English teacher has asked you to write a report giving your suggestions about:

*   what type of films should be shown
*   how often the film club should meet
*   how the film club should be advertised.

Write your **report**.

3   You see this announcement on an English-language website.

ARTICLES WANTED

What does happiness mean to you?

Tell us about the kinds of things that make you feel happy, and why?

Write us an article answering these questions.

The best articles will be posted on our website.

Write your **article**.

4   You have seen this advertisement in your local English language newspaper.

Round the world trip – Travel Competition

Do you like adventure? Would you like a chance to travel?

We need one more person to join a small group on a trip around the world.

Write to Mrs Hopkins, the organizer of the trip, telling her:

*   why you would like to go on the trip
*   what skills you have which would be useful on the trip
*   what previous experience you have of travelling (if any).

Write your **letter of application**.

LISTENING (approximately 40 minutes)

Part 1

You will hear people talking in eight different situations. For questions **1–8**, choose the best answer (**A**, **B** or **C**).

---

1   You hear a young actor talking about a colleague.
    What does he say about her?

    A She makes acting seem easy.

    B She speaks very slowly.

    C She gives him good advice.

2   You hear two friends talking about a colleague.
    What do they agree about?

    A how ambitious he is

    B how well-paid he is

    C how stressed he is

3   You hear an author talking about his new book.
    What point is he making about it?

    A It will be widely read.

    B It took a long time to write.

    C It is better than his first book.

4   You hear two friends talking about something they saw on TV.
    What did they see?

    A an advertisement

    B a comedy series

    C a documentary

5   You hear an office manager talking about her work.
How does she feel about it?

   A   confident that she can do it well

   B   interested in her new project

   C   satisfied with her staff

6   You overhear two friends talking in a restaurant.
What do they agree about?

   A   how reasonable the price is

   B   how spicy the food is

   C   how varied the menu is

7   You hear a woman talking about her neighbours' holiday photographs.
What is she doing?

   A   complaining about having to look at them

   B   admiring her neighbours' photography skills

   C   suggesting how they could be improved

8   You hear two friends talking about a concert they've just been to.
What did they find disappointing about it?

   A   the poor sound quality

   B   the seats they had booked

   C   the lack of air conditioning

Part 2

You will hear a man called Henry Lee giving a talk about the first time he went skydiving. For questions **9–18**, complete the sentences with a word or short phrase.

My first jump

Henry had his first skydiving lesson in the month of [**9**] .

Henry had to attend a talk about [**10**] before his jump.

Henry says that a [**11**] was the most important piece of

equipment he was given.

Henry was surprised that the plane the club used didn't have any

[**12**] in it.

Henry's instructor had jumped a total of [**13**] times in

the past.

Henry had brought some [**14**] with him to wear during

the jump.

Henry said he felt totally [**15**] when the plane door

was opened.

Henry uses the word [**16**] to describe the winding river he

could see below him.

Henry compares his landing to that of a [**17**] landing

on the ground.

Henry was pleased to be given a [**18**] after his jump.

Part 3

You will hear five short extracts in which students are talking about the experience of living and studying away from home. For questions **19–23**, choose from the list (**A–H**) what each student says. Use the letters only once. There are three extra letters which you do not need to use.

A   I was much younger than the other people I lived with.

B   I'm still closest to the people I grew up with.

Speaker 1   **19**

C   I found that joining a sports club helped me make friends.

Speaker 2   **20**

D   I didn't share many interests with my classmates.

Speaker 3   **21**

E   It was easier making friends at a small college.

Speaker 4   **22**

F   It was hard getting out to make friends at first.

Speaker 5   **23**

G   I'm still in touch with the people I lived with at first.

H   It was good living with people who had similar interests.

Part 4

You will hear an interview with a student athlete called Chelsea Matthews, who plays soccer for her college. For questions **24–30**, choose the best answer (**A**, **B** or **C**).

24 What impact does playing soccer have on Chelsea's life?

    A She needs private tuition from her teachers.

    B She doesn't take part in some other student activities.

    C She never gets to travel to other countries.

25 Chelsea had to start planning to be a student athlete at 16 because

    A there were many requirements that had to be met.

    B there were few colleges that offered the course she wanted.

    C there was a lot of competition for places in good colleges.

26 Chelsea is happy to return to college a month early because

    A she is pleased at the prospect of starting competitions.

    B she feels relieved to get back into a routine.

    C she realises that training is necessary.

27 When Chelsea and her team-mates finish training, they

    A can take a break by going to the movies.

    B are too tired to do very much except sleep.

    C relax with other sports teams.

28 Chelsea says if she and her team-mates miss too many classes

    A they may get poor grades and have to leave the team.

    B their professors will complain to the head of faculty.

    C the other students are understanding about the reason for their absence.

29 What problem did Chelsea herself have in keeping up with her studies?

    A She was away sick for some of her classes.

    B She had to study one subject under difficult conditions.

    C She was expected to commit herself to extra training for away games.

30 In conclusion, what does Chelsea say about being a student athlete?

    A It has taught her the importance of aiming high.

    B It has helped her decide what her future career should be.

    C It has changed her perception of the value of friendship.

SPEAKING (14 minutes)

You take the Speaking test with another candidate (possibly two candidates), referred to here as your partner. There are two examiners. One will speak to you and your partner and the other will be listening. Both examiners will award marks.

Part 1 (2 minutes)

The examiner asks you and your partner questions about yourselves. You may be asked about things like 'your home town', 'your interests', 'your career plans', etc.

Part 2 (a one-minute 'long turn' for each candidate, plus a 30-second response from the second candidate)

The examiner gives you two photographs and asks you to talk about them for one minute. The examiner then asks your partner a question about your photographs and your partner responds briefly.

Then the examiner gives your partner two different photographs. Your partner talks about these photographs for one minute. This time the examiner asks you a question about your partner's photographs and you respond briefly.

Part 3 (4 minutes)

The examiner asks you and your partner to talk together. You may be asked to solve a problem or try to come to a decision about something. For example, you might be asked to decide the best way to use some rooms in a language school. The examiner gives you some text to help you but does not join in the conversation.

Part 4 (4 minutes)

The examiner asks some further questions, which leads to a more general discussion of what you have talked about in Part 3. You may comment on your partner's answers if you wish.

Test 4

READING AND USE OF ENGLISH (1 hour 15 minutes)

Part 1

For questions **1–8**, read the text below and decide which answer (**A**, **B**, **C** or **D**) best fits each gap. There is an example at the beginning (**0**).

Mark your answers **on the separate answer sheet**.

Example:

0 **A** heart   **B** key   **C** bottom   **D** focus

0	A	B	C	D
	▬	▭	▭	▭

Memory

Memory is at the **(0)** …….... of our sense of personal identity. If we did not have memory, we would not be **(1)** …….... of our relationships with other people and would have no **(2)** …….... that we had had any past at all. And without memory we would have no knowledge on which to **(3)** …….... our present and future.

Memory **(4)** …….... of three processes: registration, retention and recall. Registration happens when we consciously notice something. Retention is the next **(5)** …….... , when we keep something we have noticed in our minds for a certain period of time. Finally, recall occurs when we actively think about some of these things that are **(6)** …….... in our minds.

Every day we are subjected to a vast **(7)** …….... of information. If we remembered every **(8)** …….... thing we had ever seen or heard, life would be impossible. Consequently, our brains have learnt to register only what is of importance.

1   **A**   familiar   **B**   aware   **C**   informed   **D**   acquainted

2   **A**   view   **B**   suggestion   **C**   belief   **D**   idea

3   **A**   base   **B**   depend   **C**   do   **D**   make

4   **A**   contains   **B**   involves   **C**   includes   **D**   consists

5   **A**   action   **B**   division   **C**   set   **D**   stage

6   **A**   seated   **B**   stocked   **C**   stored   **D**   sited

7   **A**   level   **B**   amount   **C**   extent   **D**   number

8   **A**   exact   **B**   single   **C**   one   **D**   isolated

Part 2

For questions **9–16**, read the text below and think of the word which best fits each gap. Use only **one** word in each gap. There is an example at the beginning (**0**).

Write your answers **IN CAPITAL LETTERS on the separate answer sheet.**

Example: | 0 | B | E | T | W | E | E | N | | | | | | | | | | | |

Visit to a sweets factory

Today I am visiting a sweets factory, a building squeezed **(0)** .... a railway line and a canal. **(9)** .... I watch, trucks filled with sugar arrive at the factory where this family-owned company has been making sweets for some 80 years.

Being in a factory **(10)** .... this one is exactly **(11)** .... children dream of. I am staring at huge vats of sticky liquid **(12)** .... eventually ends up as mouth-watering sweets. Every now **(13)** .... then I see a factory worker in a white coat put a sweet into her mouth.

Ailsa Kelly, granddaughter of the company owner, remembers visiting the factory as **(14)** .... child with her grandfather. 'He would take me onto the factory floor and introduce me,' she says. 'He told me, "You may work here some day." And indeed, she has, continuously, **(15)** .... 1999. The sense of family is **(16)** .... of the reasons employees are remarkably loyal to the company.

Part 3

For questions **17–24**, read the text below. Use the word given in capitals at the end of some of the lines to form a word that fits in the gap **in the same line**. There is an example at the beginning (**0**).

Write your answers **IN CAPITAL LETTERS on the separate answer sheet**.

Example: | 0 | N | E | R | V | O | U | S | | | | | | | | |

Job interviews

Most people feel rather **(0)** ……….. when they go for an interview for a new   **NERVE**

job. This is not surprising as getting a job one wants is important. People

being interviewed expect the interviewers to be **(17)** ……….. , matching   **OBJECT**

an applicant against a job **(18)** ……….. . However, what often happens in   **DESCRIBE**

reality is that the interviewers make **(19)** ……….. that are little more than   **DECIDE**

reactions to the **(20)** ……….. of the applicant.   **PERSON**

Even skilled interviewers may, without realising it, **(21)** ……….. favour   **CONSCIOUS**

people who make them feel at **(22)** ……….. . With this in mind, if you go   **EASY**

for an interview you should try to make a good impression from the start

by presenting the interviewers with the very best version of yourself,

emphasising the **(23)** ……….. of skills you have. You must appear very   **VARY**

positive and as **(24)** ……….. as possible. It is for you to convince the   **ENTHUSIASM**

interviewers that you are definitely the most suitable person for the job.

Part 4

For questions **25–30**, complete the second sentence so that it has a similar meaning to the first sentence, using the word given. **Do not change the word given.** You must use between **two** and **five** words, including the word given. Here is an example (**0**).

Example:

0   A very friendly taxi driver drove us into town.

DRIVEN

We .... a very friendly taxi driver.

The gap can be filled by the words 'were driven into town by', so you write:

Example:	**0**	*WERE DRIVEN INTO TOWN BY*

Write **only** the missing words **IN CAPITAL LETTERS on the separate answer sheet**.

---

25   'Do you know the cost of the trips?' asked Pamela.

MUCH

Pamela asked if I knew .... were.

26   During the quiz, I could not think of the correct answer to the winning question.

COME

During the quiz, I was not .... the correct answer to the winning question.

27   I promised that I would think carefully about the job offer.

GIVE

I promised .... the job offer.

28 The group continued to walk despite rain starting to fall.

EVEN

The group carried .... started to rain.

29 Almost all the tickets for next Saturday's concert have been sold.

HARDLY

There are .... for next Saturday's concert.

30 Do you think it is likely that Peter will get the job he has applied for?

CHANCE

Do you think that Peter has .... the job he has applied for?

Part 5

You are going to read an article about the video games industry. For questions **31–36**, choose the answer (**A**, **B**, **C** or **D**) which you think fits best according to the text.

Mark your answers **on the separate answer sheet**.

A career in the video games industry?

Reporter Lauren Cope finds out about working in the video games industry.

Initially populated by computer scientists and the self-taught, the video game design industry used not to offer many routes into its midst. Often, perhaps unfairly, viewed as just a hobby for young enthusiasts, the video games industry is now being taken seriously. Surprised? Industry experts aren't.

It's not easy though. Video game spin-offs that rapidly follow any new movie require dozens of team members and months of incredible skill, perseverance and intricacies. As with almost every industry, it's tricky to get into – but it is expanding. Jim Donelly, a spokesman for an online games magazine says: 'It's certainly very difficult to make much headway within big companies, or to influence any of the really big mainstream games. But the truth is, the industry needs game designers more than ever. Not just director-level people who orchestrate an entire game, but the lower-level people who design systems and individual set pieces.'

So, how can you get into such a competitive industry? Although many companies prefer people to have a degree in computer science, Jim disagrees. 'There is only one route: make games. The tools are there. You won't get a job if you haven't made something, and you won't get anywhere independently if you are not making stuff. Game design is less a job than it is a way of life. Like any creative endeavour it must be done to be real.' Another industry expert, John Field, sees other options. 'There's a lot to be said for "just *line 32* doing it", but it's really more complicated than that. There are lots of people who want to work in games, but few who measure up to the requirements of the industry these days; even fewer who have the creative talent, technical know-how, vision and entrepreneurial ability to really contribute to the ever-changing face of an evolving medium.'

Can you do it on your own? 'Perhaps, but it's pretty tricky,' says John. 'However, a good postgraduate course in games can help, plus provide a year or two of top-level support and guidance. Most games designers start their careers as programmers, or artists, progressing their way up the ladder. They are interested in all forms of entertainment media, plus have a healthy appetite for all areas of the arts and contemporary culture. They may or may not have spent a few years in the working world post-graduation, but have realised that games is going to be their "thing". They are not merely fans, but are fascinated by the future possibilities of games, and are aware of the increasing breadth and diversity of the form. And finally connections can help. This is often overlooked, but in order to get *line* ahead in games – as in many other areas – you need to network.'

The childish stereotype of the adolescent boy glued to his games console has long been replaced by the more accurate perception of a grown-up medium, grabbing our attention. Families frequently get involved on interactive consoles. Smart phones introduce a wealth of new games through apps, as well as social media. John believes there is plenty of room for expansion. 'Games have become pervasive play-things for increasingly large audiences. They are also a great way to learn things and I see this already big area as an expanding array of possibilities and opportunities.'

31 What is the writer's main point about the video games industry in the first paragraph?

   A It is reasonable to consider making a living in this field.
   B Young people's contributions to it should be appreciated.
   C It offers a relatively limited number of career options.
   D Specialists in this area have failed to value its potential.

32 What does Jim tell us about the video games industry?

   A It can be hard to decide which idea will prove successful.
   B Many designers are required to take charge of each large project.
   C It is worth recognising the value of having a long-term strategy.
   D There is room for people with different degrees of responsibility.

33 What does 'that' refer to in line 32?

   A getting a degree in computer science
   B making games
   C being independent
   D seeing other options

34 What opinion does John express in the third paragraph?

   A It is a mistake to believe that the jobs people do in the industry are easy.
   B Many people lack the qualities needed to do effective work in the industry.
   C The industry could benefit from people who have a strong desire to work in it.
   D The industry is changing too rapidly for people to keep up with it.

35 What does 'overlooked' mean in line 54?

   A not considered
   B understood
   C not used
   D required

36 In the final paragraph, we are told that

   A video games have not been effectively exploited as learning tools.
   B young people are being offered more demanding games to play.
   C people used to misunderstand the true nature of video games.
   D other technologies have forced the games industry to compete.

Part 6

You are going to read part of the autobiography of David Coulthard, who is a retired Formula One racing driver. Six sentences have been removed from the autobiography. Choose from the sentences **A–G** the one which fits each gap (**37–42**). There is one extra sentence which you do not need to use.

Mark your answers **on the separate answer sheet**.

Grand Prix driver

I'm a great believer in success, in achieving whatever goal you set on a particular day, so whether I was practising on the track or working out in the gym, I always put my heart and soul into it.

When I was learning my trade, racing on karts as a teenager, I would look after my helmet and race suit carefully. Everything had to be perfect; it was all about preparation. At 18, I progressed to Formula Ford racing, a stage before Formula One, and I'd even get the car up in the garage and polish the underside until it was gleaming. **37** But I made the point, jokingly, that if I ever rolled over in a race, my car would have the shiniest underside in history.

It may be that the environment of Formula One fuelled this obsession with neatness and cleanliness. It's a profession based on precision and exactness. If you walk around a team factory it looks like a science laboratory. **38** A Formula One factory couldn't be further from that; it's like something from another planet.

Everything is aircraft standard and quality. And so it should be. If some mega-rich potential sponsor walks into a dirty factory to find people lounging around, that doesn't make a great impression. If they walk in and everyone's working hard and there's not a speck of dust anywhere, that's another matter. **39**

Polishing my helmet was a specific ritual I had. The race helmet is an important and prized possession. When you're starting out, you only have one helmet for several years and it can be a pricey piece of kit. **40** By the time you get to Formula One, you're getting through probably a dozen or more expensive ones a year. Normally I'd never have dreamed of wearing someone else's, but I did have a problem with the front of my helmet some years ago at the Monaco Grand Prix, and just couldn't see properly. In the end I used one belonging to Nelson Piquet.

He very kindly let me keep the helmet after the race. He'd finished second in the Brazilian Grand Prix with that helmet, so it's a unique piece of history – two drivers wearing the same helmet and finishing second in different races. Four years later, Nelson said he wanted to swap another helmet with me. This was before he'd announced he was retiring, so my immediate thought was, what's with this helmet collection thing? **41** There must be something in it. So I gave him a helmet and he gave me a signed one of his.

Helmets are treasured and it's quite rare for me to give race ones to anyone. I only gave my friend Richard one recently, although we've known each other since we were five. Sometimes it's easy to forget obvious things. **42** It should be the other way round.

A I certainly took good care of mine as a result.

B You take for granted those you're closest to and you make an effort with people you hardly know.

C But it was only natural for me to be so particular about cleanliness before racing.

D Think of a motor mechanic, and you think of oil and dirt, filthy overalls, grubby fingers.

E Some people said this was ridiculous because it wasn't as if anyone was ever going to see it.

F Perhaps I should be doing it as well.

G That's why all the teams try and compete hard with each other on presentation.

Part 7

You are going to read an article about four women who have recently worked as volunteers. For questions **43–52**, choose from the women (**A–D**). The women may be chosen more than once.

Mark your answers **on the separate answer sheet**.

Which volunteer

found that there was a wide choice of opportunities?	**43**
was very aware of all aspects of natural life around her?	**44**
was warned of a possible danger?	**45**
did not achieve her ambition quite as she had expected?	**46**
thought that she had gained as much as she had given?	**47**
was shown sympathy by someone on her project?	**48**
says her family had influenced her choice of work?	**49**
says she amazed herself by what she achieved?	**50**
appreciated the flexibility of her boss?	**51**
describes the difficulties posed by the environment she was in?	**52**

Volunteers

A Teresa

For many years I had fantasised about spending December on a white, tropical beach on a remote island. I finally found my slice of paradise in the Seychelles when my dream came true last year, though not exactly in the way I had envisaged. I had been feeling burnt out from work and wanted to escape winter and learn new skills. Volunteer projects seemed a good option. Narrowing my search criteria to marine research helped cut down the thousands of options out there and I eventually joined a coral protection project to help determine the long-term impact of rising sea temperatures on the ecosystem. Within 24 hours of our group's arrival, we lived and breathed coral, not just under water but also in the camp – with 52 coral types to master and up to three research dives a day. If there was a downside, it was the seemingly endless chores in the camp, but I didn't mind. But the experience was, overall, incredible. I stretched myself beyond my wildest imagination.

B Patricia

Imagine spending the summer as I did, working on the edge of an active volcano in Hawaii. I had once been on a ranger-guided walk there with my family. I had been terrified. However, as I relaxed I slowly realised that the ranger's job was something I'd like to do too. So a few years later I applied and got a volunteer ranger job. I found living there surprisingly laid back, as well as exciting. After a crash course in geology, I was given the volunteer ranger uniform and began the job. On the first morning I found myself in front of a group of visitors. Suddenly, I was the 'authority', delivering a talk on the volcanic past and present of the islands. As a volunteer I was making the park come alive for the visitors, and they in turn made Hawaii come alive for me.

C Helen

After months of study, I wanted to get away for a bit. My dad is an artist and often does paintings of tropical birds. I'd always wanted to find out more about them. From the internet I found that a farm which breeds parrots was looking for volunteers. I arrived in the middle of a panic situation – a storm had knocked the electricity out, and the generator, needed for keeping the eggs warm, was nearly out of petrol. After visiting several garages we found some and dashed back just in time. I really enjoyed my stay. Some hosts lay down strict rules on the amount of work expected but luckily mine, Darryl, preferred to set out projects which he wanted my help with. Most of the time I did basic maintenance jobs and fed the birds. 'They can break coconuts with their beaks and they'll take your finger off so be careful,' Darryl advised. So, I chopped bananas and then used a long fork to pass the fruit in to the birds without risking my fingers.

D Kate

During my stay in Guatemala, I volunteered to work on a plantation. One day, my supervisor, René inspected my scratched hands and asked gently if I needed gloves. I gathered my strength and told him that gloves might indeed help. Then I grasped my knife and resumed my attack on the invading roots that were constantly threatening to drag the fragile new cacao plantation back into the rainforest. In the sticky red earth, everything grows – the trouble is that it is rarely what you planted. Walking through the plantation, René had to point out to me the treasured cash crops of coffee, cacao and macadamias. To my eye, they were indistinguishable from the surrounding jungle. Every day I caught glimpses of little waterfalls and vividly coloured butterflies between towering bamboo. The air was always heavy with the sound of insects. It was a great experience.

WRITING (1 hour 20 minutes)

Part 1

You **must** answer this question. Write your answer in **140–190** words in an appropriate style **on the separate answer sheet**.

1   In your English class you have been talking about animals and the environment. Now, your English teacher has asked you to write an essay.

Write an essay using **all** the notes and give reasons for your point of view.

'We should do everything we can to save animals which are in danger of disappearing from our planet.' Do you agree?

Notes

Write about:

1.   the kind of animals which are in danger

2.   the reasons for protecting these animals

3.   … (your own idea)

Write your **essay**. You must use grammatically correct sentences with accurate spelling and punctuation in a style appropriate for the situation.

Part 2

Write an answer to **one** of the questions **2–4** in this part. Write your answer in **140–190** words in an appropriate style **on the separate answer sheet**. Put the question number in the box at the top of the answer sheet.

2   You see this announcement on an English-language website.

> **ARTICLES WANTED**
>
> ## What are the most important things for young children to learn?
>
> How to make friends? Telling the truth? Or something else? Write us an article saying what things you think are important for young children to learn, and why?
>
> The best articles will be posted on our website.

Write your **article**.

3   You recently saw this notice on an English-language website called Music Live.

> **Reviews Wanted!**
>
> ## A concert I've been to
>
> Write us a review of a concert you've been to. It could be a pop, rock or classical concert, or one with a different type of music. Include information on the music, the place and the atmosphere.
>
> The best reviews will be posted on the website next month.

Write your **review**.

4   A group of English students is coming to your college. Your English teacher has asked you to write a report on **one** local tourist attraction. In your report you should:

- describe the attraction
- say what you can do there
- explain why you think students would enjoy visiting it.

Write your **report**.

LISTENING (approximately 40 minutes)

Part 1

You will hear people talking in eight different situations. For questions **1–8**, choose the best answer (**A, B** or **C**).

1   You hear a sportsperson talking about her sporting career.
    What is she going to do in the future?

    A change her career

    B become a sports writer

    C train for the next event

2   You hear two friends talking about a laboratory experiment.
    How do they both feel now?

    A anxious about the procedures they used

    B annoyed about having to repeat it

    C disappointed with the results

3   You overhear a student calling his university department.
    Why is he phoning?

    A to make a complaint

    B to find out about a course

    C to book an appointment

4   You hear two friends talking about a website.
    The man thinks that the website is

    A helpful.

    B interesting.

    C easy to use.

5 You hear a man talking about his decision to become a singer.
His mother was unhappy about it because she didn't

   A like his kind of music.

   B want him to leave education.

   C think it would suit him.

6 You overhear a man calling a TV shop.
Why is he calling?

   A to cancel an order

   B to arrange a delivery

   C to make a purchase

7 You hear two friends talking about a meal.
What do they agree about it?

   A It was expensive for the amount of food they got.

   B Some of the foods they were served didn't go well together.

   C The dishes they were given weren't cooked properly.

8 You hear a college lecturer talking to a student.
What is he doing?

   A giving encouragement

   B offering to help

   C suggesting improvements

Part 2

You will hear a girl called Kyra talking about the badminton club she belongs to. For questions **9–18**, complete the sentences with a word or short phrase.

Badminton club

Before she took up badminton, [_____ **9**] had been Kyra's

favourite sport.

People interested in joining the club are invited to what's called a

['_____' **10**] session.

Club committee members can be identified by the colour of their

[_____ **11**] at sessions.

Members of the badminton club pay a membership fee of

[£ _____ **12**] each year.

New badminton club members can use the [_____ **13**]

at Sportsworld without paying.

When new members join the club, a [_____ **14**] is given to them

as a free gift.

There is coaching for the club's [_____ **15**] on a Monday evening.

Members can look at the club's [_____ **16**] to see which

courts are free at Sportsworld.

The club's annual [_____ **17**] is its most popular social event.

New badminton club members will be offered a [_____ **18**]

at the Sportsworld café.

Part 3

You will hear five short extracts in which people are talking about why their businesses became successful. For questions **19–23**, choose from the list (**A–H**) what each speaker says. Use the letters only once. There are three extra letters which you do not need to use.

A   I don't need to employ anyone.

B   I decided to change the way I promoted the business.

Speaker 1   **19**

C   I took a business course.

Speaker 2   **20**

D   I was able to get financial backing.

Speaker 3   **21**

E   I believe in looking after my employees.

Speaker 4   **22**

F   I believe my business offers a unique service to customers.

Speaker 5   **23**

G   I learnt a lot from other business people.

H   I made changes because of customer feedback.

Part 4

You will hear a radio interview with a man called Tony Little, who makes wildlife films and works for a wildlife conservation organisation called The Nature Trust. For questions **24–30**, choose the best answer (**A**, **B** or **C**).

24 Tony thinks that the hardest challenge he faces is

    A to publicise what The Nature Trust does.

    B to expand the range of people volunteering.

    C to interest local groups in a variety of activities.

25 What does Tony think about the use of plastic?

    A He knows it will be difficult to change people's attitudes to it.

    B He worries that there is no way of preventing plastic waste.

    C He believes it causes the biggest problem to wildlife.

26 Tony hopes that his new website Nature Talk will help people learn

    A about different animal habitats.

    B how to watch animals in the wild.

    C which animals are endangered.

27 Tony says the achievement that he is most proud of is

    A helping to make a popular film.

    B doing a scientific study.

    C working on an award-winning project.

28 What disadvantage does Tony mention about having a career as a cameraman?

    A It is often badly paid.

    B It can be hard to find enough work.

    C It usually involves long hours.

29 Tony advises young naturalists that it is essential to have

    A suitable walking boots.

    B the latest photography equipment.

    C good binoculars.

30 What would Tony like to do in the future?

    A to help save the tiger and polar bear

    B to publicise the dangers facing a variety of species

    C to produce more films for TV about animals

SPEAKING (14 minutes)

You take the Speaking test with another candidate (possibly two candidates), referred to here as your partner. There are two examiners. One will speak to you and your partner and the other will be listening. Both examiners will award marks.

Part 1 (2 minutes)

The examiner asks you and your partner questions about yourselves. You may be asked about things like 'your home town', 'your interests', 'your career plans', etc.

Part 2 (a one-minute 'long turn' for each candidate, plus a 30-second response from the second candidate)

The examiner gives you two photographs and asks you to talk about them for one minute. The examiner then asks your partner a question about your photographs and your partner responds briefly.

Then the examiner gives your partner two different photographs. Your partner talks about these photographs for one minute. This time the examiner asks you a question about your partner's photographs and you respond briefly.

Part 3 (4 minutes)

The examiner asks you and your partner to talk together. You may be asked to solve a problem or try to come to a decision about something. For example, you might be asked to decide the best way to use some rooms in a language school. The examiner gives you some text to help you but does not join in the conversation.

Part 4 (4 minutes)

The examiner asks some further questions, which leads to a more general discussion of what you have talked about in Part 3. You may comment on your partner's answers if you wish.

CAMBRIDGE ENGLISH
Language Assessment
Part of the University of Cambridge

Do not write in this box

SAMPLE

Candidate Name
If not already printed, write name in CAPITALS and complete the Candidate No. grid (in pencil).

Candidate Signature

Examination Title

Centre

Supervisor:
If the candidate is ABSENT or has WITHDRAWN shade here ⊂⊃

Centre No.

Candidate No.

Examination Details

0	0	0	0
1	1	1	1
2	2	2	2
3	3	3	3
4	4	4	4
5	5	5	5
6	6	6	6
7	7	7	7
8	8	8	8
9	9	9	9

Candidate Answer Sheet

Instructions

Use a PENCIL (B or HB).

Rub out any answer you wish to change using an eraser.

Parts 1, 5, 6 and 7:
Mark ONE letter for each question.

For example, if you think **B** is the right answer to the question, mark your answer sheet like this:

0 A B̶ C D

Parts 2, 3 and 4:
Write your answer clearly in CAPITAL LETTERS.

For Parts 2 and 3 write one letter in each box. For example:

0 EXAMPLE

Part 1

1	A	B	C	D
2	A	B	C	D
3	A	B	C	D
4	A	B	C	D
5	A	B	C	D
6	A	B	C	D
7	A	B	C	D
8	A	B	C	D

Part 2

Do not write below here

9													9 1 0 u
10													10 1 0 u
11													11 1 0 u
12													12 1 0 u
13													13 1 0 u
14													14 1 0 u
15													15 1 0 u
16													16 1 0 u

Continues over ➡

FCE R

DP802

Sample answer sheet: Reading and Use of English

Part 3

17		Do not write below here: 17 · 1 · 0 · u
18		18 · 1 · 0 · u
19		19 · 1 · 0 · u
20		20 · 1 · 0 · u
21		21 · 1 · 0 · u
22		22 · 1 · 0 · u
23		23 · 1 · 0 · u
24		24 · 1 · 0 · u

Part 4

25		Do not write below here: 25 · 2 · 1 · 0 · u
26		26 · 2 · 1 · 0 · u
27		27 · 2 · 1 · 0 · u
28		28 · 2 · 1 · 0 · u
29		29 · 2 · 1 · 0 · u
30		30 · 2 · 1 · 0 · u

Part 5

31	A B C D
32	A B C D
33	A B C D
34	A B C D
35	A B C D
36	A B C D

Part 6

37	A B C D E F G
38	A B C D E F G
39	A B C D E F G
40	A B C D E F G
41	A B C D E F G
42	A B C D E F G

Part 7

43	A B C D E F
44	A B C D E F
45	A B C D E F
46	A B C D E F
47	A B C D E F
48	A B C D E F
49	A B C D E F
50	A B C D E F
51	A B C D E F
52	A B C D E F

CAMBRIDGE ENGLISH
Language Assessment
Part of the University of Cambridge

Do not write in this box

SAMPLE

Candidate Name
If not already printed, write name
in CAPITALS and complete the
Candidate No. grid (in pencil).

Candidate Signature

Examination Title

Centre

Supervisor:
If the candidate is ABSENT or has WITHDRAWN shade here ▭

Centre No.

Candidate No.

Examination Details

0	0	0	0
1	1	1	1
2	2	2	2
3	3	3	3
4	4	4	4
5	5	5	5
6	6	6	6
7	7	7	7
8	8	8	8
9	9	9	9

Candidate Answer Sheet

Instructions

Use a PENCIL (B or HB).
Rub out any answer you wish to change using an eraser.

Parts 1, 3 and **4:**
Mark ONE letter for each question.

For example, if you think **B** is the right answer to the question, mark your answer sheet like this:

Part 2:
Write your answer clearly in CAPITAL LETTERS.

Write one letter or number in each box.
If the answer has more than one word, leave one box empty between words.

For example:

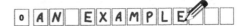

Turn this sheet over to start.

Part 1

	A	B	C
1	⊏⊐	⊏⊐	⊏⊐
2	⊏⊐	⊏⊐	⊏⊐
3	⊏⊐	⊏⊐	⊏⊐
4	⊏⊐	⊏⊐	⊏⊐
5	⊏⊐	⊏⊐	⊏⊐
6	⊏⊐	⊏⊐	⊏⊐
7	⊏⊐	⊏⊐	⊏⊐
8	⊏⊐	⊏⊐	⊏⊐

Part 2 (Remember to write in CAPITAL LETTERS or numbers)

Do not write below here

9		9 1 0 u
10		10 1 0 u
11		11 1 0 u
12		12 1 0 u
13		13 1 0 u
14		14 1 0 u
15		15 1 0 u
16		16 1 0 u
17		17 1 0 u
18		18 1 0 u

Part 3

	A	B	C	D	E	F	G	H
19	⊏⊐	⊏⊐	⊏⊐	⊏⊐	⊏⊐	⊏⊐	⊏⊐	⊏⊐
20	⊏⊐	⊏⊐	⊏⊐	⊏⊐	⊏⊐	⊏⊐	⊏⊐	⊏⊐
21	⊏⊐	⊏⊐	⊏⊐	⊏⊐	⊏⊐	⊏⊐	⊏⊐	⊏⊐
22	⊏⊐	⊏⊐	⊏⊐	⊏⊐	⊏⊐	⊏⊐	⊏⊐	⊏⊐
23	⊏⊐	⊏⊐	⊏⊐	⊏⊐	⊏⊐	⊏⊐	⊏⊐	⊏⊐

Part 4

	A	B	C
24	⊏⊐	⊏⊐	⊏⊐
25	⊏⊐	⊏⊐	⊏⊐
26	⊏⊐	⊏⊐	⊏⊐
27	⊏⊐	⊏⊐	⊏⊐
28	⊏⊐	⊏⊐	⊏⊐
29	⊏⊐	⊏⊐	⊏⊐
30	⊏⊐	⊏⊐	⊏⊐

Thanks and acknowledgements

The authors and publishers acknowledge the following sources of copyright material and are grateful for the permissions granted. While every effort has been made, it has not always been possible to identify the sources of all the material used, or to trace all copyright holders. If any omissions are brought to our notice, we will be happy to include the appropriate acknowledgements on reprinting.

Text Acknowledgements

Gizmag for the text on p. 10 adapted from 'Japan's two-stand folding bicycle' by Rick Martin, *Gizmag* 10/02/2010. Reproduced with permission; The Guardian for the text on p. 14 adapted from 'I had to make time for him: Alfred Brendel on Kit Armstrong' by Alan Rusbridger, *The Guardian* 02/06/2011, © Guardian News & Media Ltd 2011; The Guardian for the text on p. 16 adapted from 'The Blind Marathon Runner who trains alone' by Mark Russell, *The Guardian* 16/04/2012, © Guardian News & Media Ltd 2012; The Guardian for the text on p. 19 adapted from comments following 'Teachers: we don't all want to go to uni', *The Guardian* 25/06/2012, © Guardian News & Media Ltd 2012; HarperCollins Publishers Ltd for text C on p. 30 adapted from *Tunnel vision, Journeys of an Underground Philosopher*, by Christopher Ross. Reprinted with permission of HarperCollins Publishers Ltd © 2002, Christopher Ross; Immediate Media Company Ltd for the text on p. 33 adapted from 'Pushed to Extremes' by Ed Chipperfield, published in *BBC In Knowledge Magazine*, © Immediate Media Company Ltd; National Geographic Creative for the text on p. 36, adapted from 'Scottish Island Obsession' by Jim Richardson, *National Geographic* 07/06/2011, © Jim Richardson/National Geographic Creative; Financial Times Limited for the text on p. 38 adapted from 'I'm in charge of the Hollywood sign' by Richard Pigden, *Financial Times Magazine* 15/08/2010, The Financial Times Limited 2010. All Rights Reserved; The Guardian for text A on p. 41 adapted from 'Sarah Storey: 'I have jam sandwiches passed to me when I'm cycling on the road' by Laura Wakelin, *The Guardian* 20/01/2012, © Guardian News & Media Ltd 2012; The Guardian for text B on p. 41 adapted from 'Jessica Ennis: 'I'm so hungry by the end of a heptathlon that I just want to indulge' by Laura Wakelin, *The Guardian* 20/01/2012, © Guardian News & Media Ltd 2012; The Guardian for text C on p. 41 adapted from 'Louis Smith: 'I make a good roast duck. I won Ready Steady Cook with it' by Laura Wakelin, *The Guardian* 20/01/2012, © Guardian News & Media Ltd 2012; The Guardian for text D on p. 41 adapted from Keri-Anne Payne: 'Swimming is my passion. Baking comes a close second' by Laura Wakelin, *The Guardian* 20/01/2012, © Guardian News & Media Ltd 2012; Nate Nault for the text on p. 47 adapted from '10 of my favorite study abroad photos and the story behind them', http://thestudyabroadblog. com/favorite-study-abroad-photos/; Copyright © by Nate Nault. Reprinted with permission; Yale University Press for the text on p. 54 adapted from *A Little Book of Language* by David Crystal, Yale University Press, © 2011; Hodder Paperbacks for the text on p. 58 adapted from *Nobbut A Lad. A Yorkshire Childhood* by Alan Titchmarsh. Reprinted with permission of Hodder Paperbacks, © 2007; The Guardian for the text on p. 60 adapted from 'Does music help you to run faster?' by Adharanand Finn, *The Guardian* 22/04/2012, © Guardian News & Media Ltd 2012; Immediate Media Company Ltd for text A p. 63 adapted from 'Horizon: Science for Everyone' by Tom Cole, published in *Radio Times* magazine 04/11/2008, © Immediate Media Company Ltd; Telegraph Media Group for text B on p. 63 adapted from 'Orbit: Earth's Extraordinary Journey, BBC Two, review' by Andrew Marsza, *The Telegraph* 05/03/2012, Copyright © Telegraph Media Group Limited, 2012; The Independent for text C on p. 63 adapted from 'The Weekend's TV: Wonders of the Universe, Sun, BBC2 Civilization: Is the West History? Reviewed by Tom Sutcliffe', by Tom Sutcliffe, *The Independent* 07/03/2011, Copyright © The Independent 2011; Immediate Media Company Ltd for text D on p. 63 adapted from 'Channel 4 to create a bionic human in groundbreaking science documentary' by Susanna Lazarus, published in *Radio Times* magazine 25/10/2012, © Immediate Media Company Ltd; Claire Morris for the text on p. 70 adapted from 'My Life as a Student Athlete', http://collegecandy. com/2010/07/30/my-life-as-a-student-athelete/; Copyright © by Claire Morris. Reprinted with permission; Quercus Publishing Plc for the text on p. 74 adapted from *Big Ideas in Brief* by Ian Crofton, Quercus Publishing Plc, © 2012. Reproduced with permission; John Lees for the text on p. 77 adapted from 'Personality stakes' by John Lees, *Metro*, Manchester 18/09/2012, © Metro; The Independent for the text on p. 77 adapted from 'How games have grown up to be a serious career aspiration' by Lauren Cope, *The Independent* 16/10/2012 © Copyright © The Independent 2012; Orion Books and World Famous Group for the text on p. 82 adapted from *Grand Prix Driver* by David Coulthard, © 2007, Orion Books and World Famous Group Ltd on behalf of David Coulthard with permission; The Guardian for text A on p. 85, adapted from 'Time Out not Time Off; Volunteering in Paradise by Teresa Machan, *The Guardian* 21/08/2010, © Guardian News & Media Ltd 2010; The Guardian for text B on p. 85 adapted from 'Eco holidays: Pass me that machete', *The Guardian* 19/09/2009, © Guardian News & Media Ltd 2009.

Photo acknowledgements

Key: T = Top, B = Below.

p. 38: Alamy/©Terry Harris; p. C1 (T): Getty Images/The Image Bank/Alistair Berg; p. C1 (B): Alamy/© Clynt Garnham Sport; p. C2 (T): Getty Images/The Image Bank/Peter Cade; p. C2 (B): Corbis/cultura/©Simon McComb; p. C4 (T): Getty Images/Photodisc/Andersen Ross; p. C4 (B): Getty ImagesE+/Nikki Bidgood; p. C5 (T): Corbis/©John Smith; p. C5 (B): Getty Images/Bloomberg/Chris Ratcliffe; p. C7 (T): Getty Images/Digital Vision/Briony Campbell; p. C7 (B): Getty Images/Flickr/Layland Masuda; p. C8 (T): Getty Images/Folio Images/ Lisa Bjorner; p. C8 (B): Getty Images/The Image Bank/Erik Von Weber; p. C10 (T): Getty Images/hemis.fr/Camille Moirenc; p. C10 (B): Alamy/©Kathy deWitt; p. C11 (T): Thinkstock/Purestock; p. C11 (B): Getty Images/Stone/Peter Dazeley.

The recordings which accompany this book were made at dsound, London.

Visual materials for the Speaking test

What do you think the people are enjoying about these football games?

1A

1B

What might be good or bad for the people about travelling in these ways?

1C

1D

1E

The best way to buy

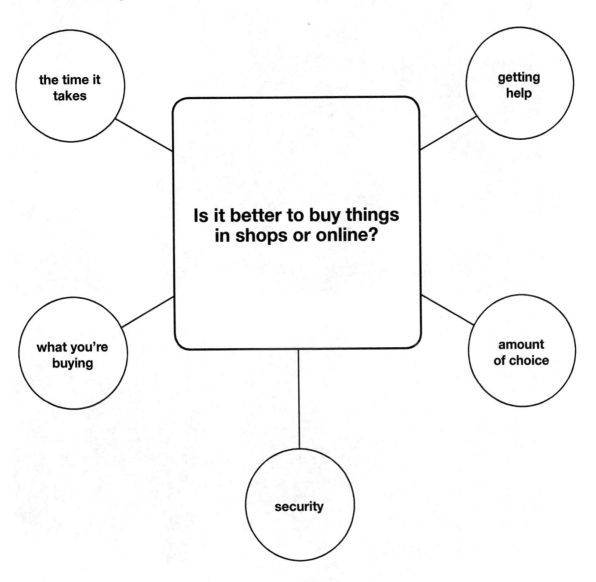

Why do you think the people are taking photographs in these situations?

2A

2B

What might be difficult for the people about doing these jobs?

2C

2D

2E

Television

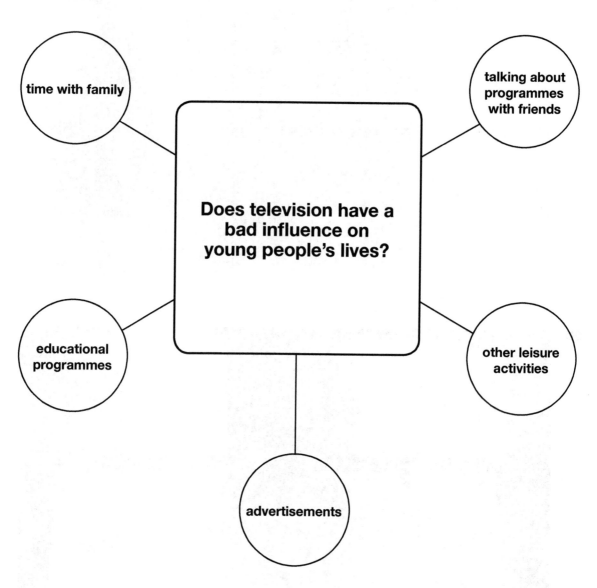

What are the people enjoying about doing these things in the evening?

3A

3B

Why have the families decided to do these things together in their free time?

3C

3D

3E

Television

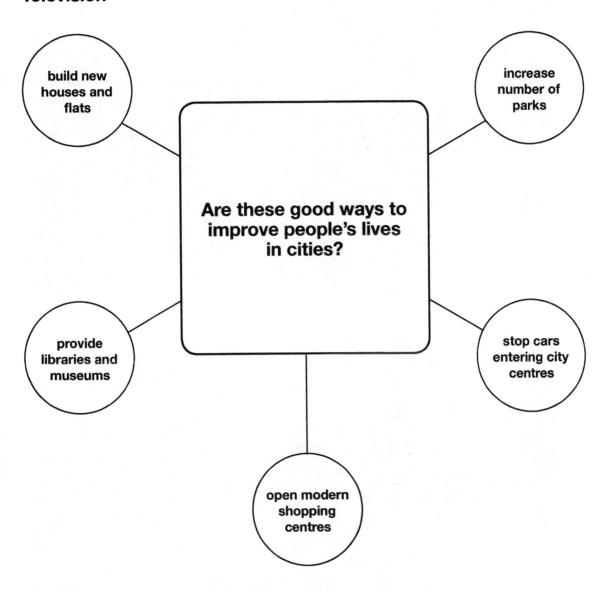

build new houses and flats

increase number of parks

Are these good ways to improve people's lives in cities?

provide libraries and museums

stop cars entering city centres

open modern shopping centres

Why have the people chosen to spend time in these different places in the city?

4A

4B

What might the people enjoy about their special day?

4C

4D

4E

Important things in life

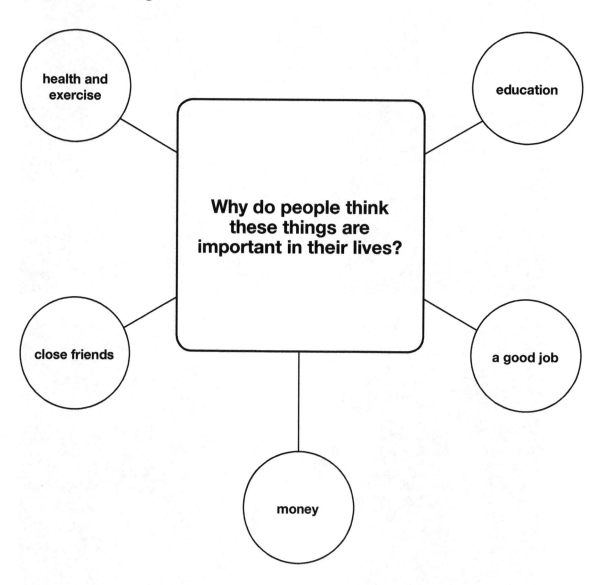